Redeeming the Season

FOCUS ON THE FAMILY®

Redeeming the Season

Simple Ideas for a Memorable and Meaningful CHRISTMAS

Kim Wier & Pam McCune

Tyndale House Publishers, Inc.
Wheaton, Illinois

Redeeming the Season
Copyright © 2002 by Kim Wier and Pam McCune
All rights reserved. International copyright secured.

ISBN: 1-58997-302-X   **3 9082 08880 6511**

A Focus on the Family book published by
Tyndale House Publishers, Wheaton, Illinois 60189

TYNDALE is a registered trademark of Tyndale House Publishers, Inc. Tyndale's
quill logo is a trademark of Tyndale House Publishers, Inc.

All Scripture quotations, unless otherwise indicated, are taken from the *Holy
Bible, New International Version*®. NIV®. Copyright © 1973, 1978, 1984 by
International Bible Society. Used by permission of Zondervan Publishing
House. All rights reserved. Scripture quotations marked (NASB) are taken from
the *New American Standard Bible*®. Copyright The Lockman Foundation 1960,
1962, 1963, 1968, 1971, 1972, 1973, 1975, 1977, 1995. Used by permission.
(www.Lockman.org).

Editors: Marianne Hering and Kathy Davis
Cover design: Kurt Birky
Cover photo: Photodisc
Cover copy: Joy Olson
Authors' photo: Sherry Braden Photography

Library of Congress Cataloging-in-Publication Data
   Wier, Kim.
     Redeeming the season : simple ideas for a memorable and meaningful
Christmas / Kim Wier & Pam McCune.
       p. cm.
     ISBN 1-58997-302-X
   Christmas. I. McCune, Pam. II. Title.
     BV45 . W53 2002
     263'.915—dc21

                                                              2002009379

Printed in the United States of America
1 2 3 4 5 6 7 8 9 / 11 10 09 08 07 06 05

CONTENTS

DEDICATION

Foremost to our Savior, the Lord Jesus Christ,
Who is worthy to be praised

To the family on which I experiment: Tony, Chase, Bailey, and
Hannah. Your smiles redeem my days. Your love overwhelms
my heart. Indeed my lines have fallen in pleasant places.
—Kim

To my three musketeers:
Jerry, my husband, best friend, and loyal warrior.
Madison, my daughter, lover of words, and delighter in truth.
Connor, my son, lover of action, and tenderhearted friend.
—Pam

ACKNOWLEDGMENTS

"With humility of mind, let each of you regard one another as more important than himself; do not merely look out for your own personal interests, but also for the interests of others. Have this attitude in yourselves which was also in Christ Jesus . . ."
Philippians 2:3-5, NASB

SPECIAL THANKS FROM KIM

How I thank God for those in my life who have looked to my interests out of a heart of love:

Linda Bailey. A more committed mom could not exist. Thank you for teaching me that a big life comes through what you choose to make of the little things. You are and always will be the generous woman I aspire to become.

My family at Grace Bible Church in Nacogdoches, Texas. Thank you for modeling Christ to me. It is an honor to grow in grace with you.

Mark Maddox of Focus on the Family. Thank you for your kindness, encouragement, and friendship. And thank you for giving me the opportunity to be a small part of a ministry that has been a big part of our family's life.

Bible Study Fellowship, International (BSF). What an incredible blessing it has been to be taught the Word of God under the stewardship of this Bible study. Thank you for your faithfulness to the Scriptures.

Pam McCune. Your tender heart for God and your passion for walking with Him at any cost are your greatest gifts of friendship to me. As Anne would say, "We are kindred spirits."

Tony Wier. Thank you for daily looking to the interests of our family, so often over your own. I love you.

SPECIAL THANKS FROM PAM

Barbara Clarkson. Thank you, Mom, for giving me "The Blessing" and painting a picture for me that I could write a book. You have given me more than you will ever know.

Frank Clarkson. Thank you, Dad, for demonstrating that anything is possible. You have stepped out and accomplished more than I could imagine. Oh how I love watching you give . . . from collecting Coke bottles to building a '68 Mustang.

Cam Sanders. Thank you, Sis, for helping me step out and enjoy life. You have taught me to laugh and to take hold of life. I am ready to go anywhere with you.

Thank you, Hayley, Heather, Shaun, Kyle, Steve, Marilyn, David, Jerry Sr., and Sue for always being there as family.

Kim Wier. Thank you for being my giant slayer, for leading the charge, and for pursuing the Savior.

Thank you to all the women from the last 20 years who have studied the Bible with me. You are my kindred spirits who have listened, laughed, and cried with me. I love savoring the Savior with you . . . Angela, Julie, Jenn, the Women of Grace Bible Church, and the many staff and students of Campus Crusade for Christ I have learned from these 20 years.

INTRODUCTION

*I*t happens. Just like clockwork Christmas arrives and once again I scarcely recognize my neighborhood. Up and down our street, strands of lights shine from rooftops and twinkle on trees proudly displayed in front windows. Smoke billows from fireplaces and lighted holiday characters decorate the yards. Year after year, the transformation of our ordinary neighborhood into a magical wonderland heralds the arrival of the holiday season—and with it the inevitable struggles with anxiety, debt, sleepless nights, and unwanted pounds. No wonder more and more moms dread the Christmas season.

While children happily make out their wish lists, moms' to-do lists explode; they no longer fit on the back of a deposit slip. By December 1, any responsible mother is halfway through a box of legal pads after whittling down stacks of sticky notes. After all, this holiday stuff is serious business. It requires stamina, ingenuity, and the ability to maneuver through large shopping crowds in a single bound. Christmas is not for wimps. Only the strong survive, and they do it by spending more time in the stores than with their families—and then more time at the office to pay off the stores.

For all that effort, we are rewarded with a Christmas experience that pales in comparison to a Hallmark commercial. Of course we cry when we watch those ads. We're overwhelmed that TV actors are having a more meaningful holiday than we are. We have been defrauded into thinking that a balanced Christmas is buying the right card to go on top of a very expensive gift.

I ought to know. Not too many years ago I bought into that philosophy hook, line, and sinker. The first clue that I had gone overboard came Christmas morning when my five-year-old son asked, "Do we have to open more presents?" On Christmas Eve we had loaded him with enough loot to give Toys "R" Us competition, and we had more waiting when he awoke Christmas day. All he wanted was to build with his new LEGO blocks, but instead I stood over him with yet another package. "Straighten up, Son. I waited in line for an hour to buy this one. Come on, open it and smile for the camera!" Then his little brother and sister were given the same treatment. By the time it was all over, everyone was exhausted, and my two-year-old was buried alive under an avalanche of crumpled wrapping.

When the mess was eventually swept away, so was our Christmas. It had all been wrapped up in colored paper and ribbons, and when they were gone, nothing remained except toys that would be missing their pieces in less than a week. That's when I realized three significant truths: First, gift bags are the greatest invention since the microwave oven. Second, small children should be accounted for before leaving the Christmas trash beside the curb. Third, and probably the greatest epiphany of all, it takes more than a Visa card with a high credit limit to ensure a meaningful Christmas.

But what exactly does it take? After all, my folks gave me wonderful holiday experiences, and they couldn't even shop online. And even if they could have, gifts are not what I remember about Christmas. In fact, of all the packages I received over the years, I can specifically recall only three.

The first was a harmonica I secretly unwrapped while everyone was outside. I carefully loosened the tape and peeked inside. For the next two weeks I enjoyed harboring my sneaky little secret, but when Christmas Eve came and I had to act surprised, I was miserable with guilt.

I also never forgot the beauty-shop doll I was given in fourth grade. That was the year I had my first crush. I practiced hairstyles and makeup on that doll's head for hours so that one day I could look beautiful for Danny Marshall.

It wasn't until my eighteenth Christmas I realized what I really needed. That's when I received the third most memorable gift: my very first padded bra. Too bad Danny didn't stick around to see the new me.

I know that there were bigger gifts, like bikes and stereos and dozens of stuffed animals, but they were quickly forgotten. Which makes me wonder: How many gifts under our tree will my children remember? Probably not many, yet shopping seemed to be the center of our holiday experience.

I don't remember shopping very much as a child, but I do remember almost every Christmas present we made. There were papier-mâché angels and a decoupage picture purse for Grandma Ann. Grandpa Jay always got black walnut divinity, and Grandma Winifred received a terrarium complete with a green ceramic frog—seventies style. Was she ever surprised! Grandpa Jay was always there to catch those moments on his Brownie camera or eight-millimeter projector. He captured dress-up at Grandma Winifred's vanity, countless card games with our cousins, and some of every holiday dinner. I relive those moments every time I watch his films.

At Grandpa Ellis and Grandma Ann's I helped make Grandma's famous marshmallow cream fudge. My favorite part was putting it out in the cold Oklahoma snow to cool. When it was ready, Grandpa always said it was the best fudge he'd ever had. Afterward, we spent the afternoon playing Monopoly with my dad while Grandma Ann did her magic in the kitchen.

Her holiday dinner was always the same—pot roast with potatoes and carrots served on the good china. It was a Christmas tradition, just like placing the star of Bethlehem on the top of the tree, like setting out the nativity set in the family room, and like hearing the Bible's Christmas story on Christmas Eve. My memories bring back people I love and moments I treasure. The best things about my Christmases past can't be bought because they are priceless.

And while my childhood Christmases pointed me in the direction of a meaningful holiday, it was the Bible that drew me the map. Creating a significant celebration means following the pattern of the first Christmas by focusing on the three things on which God focused—a family, a message, and a Savior.

Matthew's gospel reveals this threefold blueprint:

> This is how the birth of Jesus Christ came about: His mother Mary was pledged to be married to Joseph, but before they came together, she was found to be with child through the Holy Spirit. Because Joseph her husband was a righteous man and did not want to expose her to public disgrace, he had in mind to divorce her quietly.
>
> But after he had considered this, an angel of the LORD appeared to him in a dream and said, "Joseph son of David, do not be afraid to take Mary home as your wife, because what is conceived in her is from the Holy Spirit. She will give birth to a son and you are to give him the name Jesus, because he will save his people from their sins. . . .
>
> When Joseph woke up, he did what the angel of the LORD commanded him and took Mary home as his wife (Matthew 1:18-21, 24).

This simple yet holy family was at the heart of Christmas 2,000 years ago. Our families, as different as they are from Jesus' family, can be at the heart of Christmas today. During the holidays, we can set apart our family time, recommitting to one another and enjoying one another as a gift our heavenly Father has given. A meaningful Christmas means setting aside time to invest in your family relationships.

Christmas also originated around a message, which was given to season the world with truth. Luke tells about the role of John the Baptist, the first to herald the news of God's own Son. "[John] will go on before the LORD . . . to make ready a people prepared for the LORD" (1:17). Matthew 3:1-11 reveals the second part of the same message: "John the Baptist came, preaching in the Desert of Judea and saying, 'Repent, for the kingdom of heaven is near. . . . I baptize you with water for repentance. But after me will come one who is more powerful. . . . He will baptize you with the Holy Spirit and with fire.' "

God's Christmas plan included a messenger so that all people might be ready to receive His greatest gift—Jesus Christ. What an unspeakable privilege to carry on the work John began by also sharing the Christmas message with our friends and family "to make ready a people prepared for the LORD."

At Christmastime the name of Jesus hangs in the air, even in the most unlikely places. It is the perfect opportunity to season our surroundings with the message of God's love, offering others the hope of a meaningful Christmas.

Greatest of all, the heart of Christmas is in savoring the Savior Himself and appreciating His glory and greatness. Again, it is Scripture that focuses us on Christ Himself: "The Word became flesh and made his dwelling among us. We have seen his glory, the glory of the One and Only, who came from the Father, full of grace and truth" (John 1:14). And "For God so loved the world that he gave his one and only Son, that whoever believes in him shall not perish but have eternal life. For God did not send his Son into the world to condemn the world, but to save the world through him" (John 3:16-17).

The miracle of that first Christmas was God's way of giving

us a Savior, Immanuel, God with us. Jesus came that we might know Him and the Father who sent Him.

Certainly, there is room in our holiday celebrations for giving gifts that express our love for others, but there is room for so much more. Does your Christmas celebration include sanctifying and setting apart your family, seasoning your surroundings, and savoring your Savior? If not, this year you can redeem the holiday season.

This book is filled with creative, fresh ideas designed to help you bring balance and fullness to your Christmas celebration in those three areas. Choose one or two ideas from each section and see how they fit your family. If you like them, make them a yearly tradition. If not, try others until you feel you have balanced these three crucial elements of the season.

You will find that these ideas are founded on the principle that simple is better. There is no minimum-skills test required to successfully use this book. So if you are craft challenged like me, there is no need to run screaming from the room. There are no blueprints for building a nativity set from Popsicle sticks and chewing gum. If you really like that kind of stuff, however, you will find a few ideas that allow you to fire up the old glue gun and whip out the paint box. Even those, though, are goof-proof, so the rest of us can relax. They also do not require much in the way of financial resources. What are required are a willing family and a heart set on creating a meaningful Christmas.

Remember, though, your family does not have to be like mine, or anyone else's, to find ideas here that fit your life. Every family has its unique challenges in building a meaningful holiday. Growing up, I faced the challenge of experiencing a joyful holiday amidst my parents' divorce, my mother's struggles with single parenting, and eventually holidays as a blended family. Each one of those seasons required some thought and a little bit of creativity on my mom's part to ensure that our focus was on the things worth celebrating.

One way she did this was by establishing traditions. Every year, even when it was just my sister, my mom, and me, we made homemade ornaments and a construction paper chain for the tree. They were small things, but they were our small things and they made Christmas special.

Whether you are a single parent, grandparents, foster parents, a blended family, a family with one child, or a family with six, the ideas in this book will help you create a holiday that celebrates your family's unique makeup, cultural identity, and ethnic heritage. There are 18 original ideas in all, but before you get the impression that I am some Christmas superwoman, let me say, "It ain't so!" I am a classic underachiever. So to present you with a variety of amazing ideas, I recruited an overachieving partner, Pam McCune. Each idea presented has been created and adopted by either Pam's family or my own, and in some cases both. Let me make clear, however, that neither of us implements all of these ideas every year. If you find yourself tempted to try, put down the book immediately and seek professional help. Our book is meant to be a buffet for you to pick and choose from, not an all-you-can-eat special. So choose your favorites and remember that you can always come back for more.

We have tried to set the stage for you by sharing some of our experiences with these traditions. You will see that while we have been best friends for 15 years, we approach things very differently. While my life is characterized by spontaneity and humor, Pam's could be described as thoughtful and planned. Yet for both of us, building spiritually rich family traditions is a priority.

A truly significant Christmas would never be possible, however, without adding one more thing—a heart wholly committed to the Lord Jesus Christ. "Redeeming Your Heart," the last section of this book, follows the life of one woman who discovered the secret to intimate fellowship with her Lord and Savior. Through her story, we too will discover "the one thing needed" to live a life fully committed to Jesus. So no matter which ideas you choose to add to your family Christmas this year, take time to meet and learn from this woman. May her life and our book inspire you to set aside the shopping list and focus on redeeming the season.

Your Kindred in Spirit,

Kim

Sanctify Your Family

He is the image of the invisible God, the firstborn over all creation.
For by him all things were created: things in heaven and on earth,
visible and invisible, whether thrones or powers or rulers or
authorities; all things were created by him and for him.
He is before all things, and in him all things hold together.
—Colossians 1:15-17

ORNAMENT BOXES

Protecting Kim's Collection

*D*uring my junior year of college, I put up my first Christmas tree in my first apartment. I bought a few strands of lights, but couldn't afford new decorations. I had a plan to secure some, however. I went home to visit my parents just before Christmas. While I was there, I made what I thought was a simple request: I asked to take the ornaments I had made as a child and put them on my tree.

From my parents' reaction, you would have thought I had asked them to donate a kidney. My mother looked particularly stricken. "Your ornaments?" she questioned. "Those belong on our family tree."

After a day's cajoling, she agreed to part with just a few. But when she got the box down and we began to reminisce about each ornament, her resolve wavered. She had treasured those homemade trinkets for 15 years. She wasn't about to entrust them to a 20 year old who couldn't remember where she'd put her car keys. I left with a box of store-bought Christmas balls, and $20 to buy myself some new decorations.

That was 17 years ago. Now, my Christmas tree is full of ornaments that my children have made over the past 13 years. Like my mother, I wouldn't consider parting with even one of those priceless treasures, and so I developed a plan to ensure that I won't have to.

Several years ago, when the local hobby store was having a sale, I purchased three small cardboard trunks, one for each of my children. After securing brass nameplates on each box, I presented my children with their personalized ornament trunks. Then we were ready for our newest family tradition, Ornament Night.

Ornament Night inaugurates our holiday festivities every year. That's when we choose a night and begin by going out for a special family dinner. Then it's off to the stores so that each person can select a special ornament for his or her personal collection. We give the kids the freedom to select whatever ornaments are meaningful to them, as long as they stay within the price limits. We all try to choose something that will remind us of a significant event from the past year. For example, in 1999 my oldest son, Chase, began tennis lessons, so he picked an ornament that had a tennis racket on it. His sister, Hannah, chose a horse to remind her of riding lessons and Bailey, our middle son and TV addict, selected a mini channel changer.

When each one has chosen an ornament, we stop for hot chocolate before heading home. It is a great night that sets the priority of a season of family solidarity. The added bonus is that as the years go by, my children are building their collection of ornaments that they will take with them when they leave the nest, ensuring, of course, that my homemade collection stays intact. Until then, they have the joy of opening their trunk, year after year, and recalling the memory that each ornament represents.

TIPS FOR CREATING YOUR ORNAMENT NIGHT

❉ Ornament Night can be anytime before you decorate your tree. Whatever night you choose, to make this an anticipated event it's best to plan for the same date every year. The holidays will be busy, and if a time is not set aside early you may find fitting it in difficult. If an unexpected conflict does arise, postpone your outing until everyone in the family can be there.

❋ We enjoy making an entire night out of our ornament hunt, but if you choose not to go out for dinner, try to stop for hot drinks or ice cream so that your family time is extended.

❋ When you get home, use a fine-point permanent marker to date each ornament with the last two digits of the year. We also put each person's initials on the ornament so that over time there will be no confusion about an ornament's ownership.

❋ Be sure to have some wrapping tissue handy so that breakable ornaments can be stored securely in the trunks.

❋ If your younger children bring home several pieces of original holiday artwork and ornaments from school, add the extras to their trunks. When they are older, they will be able to hang handmade decorations on their trees without taking from your supply.

❋ You may want to supplement their collection in one of these ways: (1) Give an ornament as a gift that celebrates your family's unique ethnic or cultural heritage, (2) surprise them in the middle of the year with a keepsake ornament to commemorate a milestone or event, or (3) give a memorial ornament in remembrance of a loved one.

MEMENTO TREE

Pam's Pampered Plants

*n*o matter how hard I work with indoor plants, I have yet to keep one alive. My friend Deborah doesn't understand how this can happen, but then she has a thumb five shades of green.

Since she lived just four houses away, I would call on her every time I had a plant crisis. She diagnosed my black spot, powdery mildew, and lace bugs. I was sad when her family decided to move across town, not only because she wouldn't be a neighbor, but also because my poor plants would be left at my mercy.

The only good thing that came of her moving was that she offered to leave me her huge potted umbrella tree. Under her care this tree was seven feet tall, with a multistalked trunk woven together magnificently. It had three strong limbs that branched out in different directions sporting a crop of glossy green leaves. What a treasure she was giving me.

It was so pleasant, day after day, to enjoy a little of the outdoors in my house. I was surprised, though, by how many leaves it shed. I reasoned that it was just one of the little inconveniences of nurturing a lovely indoor tree. So day after day I raked leaves from my carpet, until one day I looked up and noticed that there were more leaves on the floor than on the branches.

My tree—Deborah's tree—was dead. Another houseplant sacrificed. I cringed. How would I tell my friend? Should I cancel the plans to have them for dinner that night so she wouldn't see the tragic scene, or just hide the lifeless body somewhere inconspicuous? I decided to camouflage it on my back porch behind the lucky outdoor survivors.

A month after its death, my parents came to visit and I found my mom outside examining my latest horticultural failure. "What a great tree, Pam," she said, inspired by its sprawling but dead branches. She suggested that I find a way to put it to use.

Just what I needed, one more obsolete item in my house—and not just any item, but a large dead tree. Only the day before, I had resolved to get rid of useless things. I had begun streamlining by going through closets, getting rid of anything not earning its keep. I even went through all my children's artwork from school and church. If it wasn't a masterpiece, out it went. Now I was being encouraged to find a place for a seven-foot dead tree. Just as we were brainstorming a rather sparse list of ideas, I heard screams of anguish coming from the kitchen. As I turned the corner, expecting to see someone dying or at least bleeding, I found, instead, my eight-year-old daughter holding the artwork I had carefully filed in the trash can. She was crying as she held her self-portrait made at Vacation Bible School. "Mom, why are my pictures in the trash?"

There was nothing to say except, "Madison, there must have been a big mistake." *And I was the one who made it.* With haste we rescued her work from the garbage. Now I had a dead tree to deal with and a year's worth of artwork. That's when the idea hit me.

I brought the tree back in the house and got out a roll of yarn, a hole-punch, and the big stack of artwork. Together, my children and I hung each masterpiece on the branches of the tree. Madison placed her self-portrait, marred by only a small smudge of spaghetti sauce, on the highest branch, as a reminder of the "accident." Connor found the perfect branch to hold his heavy pumpkin painting and another for his ABC page. What once was a dead tree, a product of my failure, became a place to display my children's successes. That is how our Memento Tree was born.

As the seasons change, instead of dropping leaves from its branches, we see the changing shades of artwork. My favorite season, though, is Christmas. The tree's branches are loaded with ornaments Madison and Connor make at school, cards we receive, and pictures they create. Nothing gets filed in the trash, at least not until it has had its moment of glory on the Memento Tree.

TIPS FOR CREATING YOUR MEMENTO TREE

You don't have to wait for a houseplant to die to create a Memento Tree.

* If you have access to a wooded area, take a small handsaw or limb cutters and go on an adventure to locate a Memento Tree. Look for a multibranched sapling or a branch on a larger tree with many "fingers"; either should be suitable for hanging art. Consider how much room you have and choose a tree or branch that will work well in that space.

* If you are unable to cut one from the woods, visit a local nursery and ask if you may have a dead tree they are going to discard.

* To secure your tree or branch in a planter, visit a hobby or flower shop and purchase some putty and a thick block of florist Styrofoam that will support the branch when it is full.

* Firmly stick the putty in the bottom of a heavy planter. (A ceramic planter will work well.) Then press the Styrofoam into the putty. It will work best if the Styrofoam fits tightly into the planter.

✳ After trimming the branch to the size you desire, push the trunk into the Styrofoam all the way to the bottom of the planter.

✳ Camouflage the foam with moss that can be purchased from the hobby store, or wrap decorative material around the base of the trunk. You can change this to match the seasons.

✳ If you really want to dress up the tree, paint it with gold or silver spray paint or add a string of lights.

✳ When you are ready to display an item, use a hole-punch to put a hole in one corner and then string seasonally colored yarn or ribbon through the whole. Tie it off with a knot or bow.

✳ Now you are ready to display your family's Christmas treasures.

✳ Great news—you do not have to put the Memento Tree away. You can change the artwork for each season—Christmas, Valentine's, Easter, July 4th, and so on. Display back-to-school work if there's no special occasion. When it's time to change decorations, just put your children's keepsake artwork in a large envelope, mark the year on it, and save the envelope in any kind of file cabinet you choose—but preferably not file 13.

✳ Other ideas for the Memento Tree: photos of family members who live far away; names or photos of missionaries you want to pray for; prayer requests; words of praise for kind things that your children have done.

✳ Make your Memento Tree a birthday tree. On each person's birthday, use the tree to display baby and growing-up pictures, special love messages and prayers, and cards that arrive in the mail.

KEEPSAKE CHRISTMAS CARDS
Kim's Card Caper

every Christmas our family receives several types of greetings from relatives and friends. Some send newsletters filled with interesting tidbits about the previous year. "Little Suzy lost her first tooth, and little Johnny made the all-star baseball team." They usually read like an Ozzie and Harriett family résumé. They are cute and interesting, but we never feel like we are getting the whole scoop.

If we were to chronicle our entire year, I don't think I could give a 100-percent positive report with a clear conscience. I would feel compelled to tell about Suzy's terrible twos and Johnny's C in spelling. And did I mention I wrecked the car last summer? Would anyone want to read about that at Christmastime? I wouldn't. And even if I did include only the good stuff, when you have kids, the year is full of so many monumental moments it would take a five-page report to include all the crucial information. So, for our friends' sakes, our Christmas greetings do not go out as family newsletters.

We also find that every year our box is stuffed with photographic holiday wishes. I love getting these, especially when someone we seldom get to see sends them. We might send out such a card from our family if it weren't for my "developmental" problem. You see, there are currently 17 rolls of unprocessed film scattered throughout my house, dating as far back as three years. I can never remember to take them to be developed. And when I do, it is usually six weeks before I remember to pick them up. Our Christmas cards wouldn't arrive until Valentine's Day if I attempted including a photo.

That left us with just one very ordinary option when it came to sending our holiday greetings—store-bought cards. Don't misunderstand, store-bought cards are a very respectable way to wish others a happy holiday. It's just that I can never find boxed cards that convey what our family would want to say. "Merry Christmas," "happy holidays," and "season's greetings" are not the most original thoughts ever expressed. And if our family is anything, we like to think we are original.

There was only one answer for us. We would have to make original cards, something that revealed the heart of the Wiers to our family and friends. Something like, "Roses are red, violets are blue. There was a baby in the manger born just for you."

My husband, Tony, and I write those clever quips, but the artwork is left to the kids. Each one designs a card in his or her one-of-a-kind way. Sometimes we pick a theme or a Bible verse for the year, and sometimes we let them pick their own. Either way, each card is distinctive and wonderfully original. When they are complete, we scan each design into the computer and print them on card stock. Since we have three kids, we send each one's artwork to a third of the people on our list.

The kids love showcasing their work, but more than that, we have involved our entire family in the process of sending Christmas greetings to those we know and love.

TIPS FOR CREATING KEEPSAKE CHRISTMAS CARDS
❋ Have each child design his or her card on scratch paper before creating the final copy.

- ❄ Set out supplies ahead of time. Use bright colors for better scanning or copying. Markers, pens, and pencils should be available. Also set out rulers, a dictionary, and a Bible.
- ❄ Pick a theme for the year that everyone can work from, or choose a Bible verse that will be used on each card.
- ❄ Be sure to allow children to sign and date their design in a corner of the card.
- ❄ Allow your kids to send their particular design to their friends and teachers, as well as those on your regular list.
- ❄ If you do not suffer from the same "development" problem I do, include a family photo in the envelope.
- ❄ If you don't have a scanner and publisher program on your computer, find a quick-print business to make them for you.
- ❄ If you do have the equipment to make cards at home, be sure to print them on card stock in a standard envelope size. A stationery or office-supply store will offer several size choices.
- ❄ Be sure to save the original artwork. Frame them for a keepsake collection that can be displayed every year at Christmas. As time passes, your family will love looking back at their designs.

TABLE TALK

Pam's Family Therapy

*W*hen I was growing up, my family sat around the dinner table and talked about the events of the day. It was during these memorable conversations that we discussed such things as which cat my mom accidentally ran over that day. As she knocked them off one by one, our alley became a graveyard and dinner became grief therapy. Although it is an unusual dinner topic for most families, discussing death was typical for us.

Dinner was also the time we practiced our counseling skills, like when we encouraged my sister, Cam, to "get back in the saddle" after running the car through the garage. Our words of wisdom helped her regain confidence to get behind the wheel again. At other times dinner was for brainstorming about where the hamster might be hiding or where we would spend our summer vacation. The topics varied, but dinnertime allowed us to come together as a family.

This habit has been much harder to establish with my husband and children, since our busy pace keeps us on the run. Sit-down family dinners are few and far between, and when we do come together for a meal, our conversations are often a loud, fast battle for who gets to talk the most.

Seeing that we needed to slow down and make communication a priority, I started a new family tradition to keep the conversations focused. We call it Table Talk. My favorite thing about Table Talk is that it doesn't require a lot of planning. While cooking, I come up with a question that our family is to answer during dinner. Sometimes they are general questions like, "What was a highlight of your day?" Other times they are more specific: "If you could redo anything today, what would it be?" Taking into account the events of any given day, I customize the questions. Then each person is given the opportunity to answer—without interruption. I am amazed that something as simple as focusing my family on one topic has resulted in less chaos and more sharing. We laugh. We listen. We learn.

Special occasions give opportunities for variety. My favorite variation is Christmas Table Talk. Each person in our family writes a question he or she wants to ask about Christmas. We mix spiritual and not-so-spiritual questions together, but we ask only one each night.

The first question Madison asked was "What's the favorite gift you have ever given someone else?" Connor's first question was "What's your favorite Christmas candy?" Jerry asked, "Share about some of your favorite smells of Christmas." His, of course, was the smell of turkey coming out of the oven. And I wanted to know, "If you could be any character in the Christmas story except Jesus, who would you be?"

Table Talk requires almost no preparation, and so it is a tradition that can easily be added to others you already have.

Table Talk tips
Setting the stage for Table Talk:
❋ Make a commitment to fit Table Talks in at least twice a week. If you have older children, have them pencil in those days on their calendars so they know that it is a night set aside for a family meal.

❋ Make an ordinary dinner feel special by eating at the table on real plates or lighting candles and using cloth napkins.

❋ Even if it is just providing background noise, turn off the stereo or TV so that you can give one another undivided attention.

❋ Make a commitment not to answer the phone during family dinnertime. If it is just too tempting, turn off the ringer and check your messages after dinner.

❋ If you absolutely have no time to cook, but you can eat together, bring food in, but put it on real plates. Fast food containers make things seem rushed.

❋ Begin the conversation even as you are getting help with dinner preparations and table setting.

❋ Expect each person to display courteous manners. We continually remind our children that manners are not for them; manners are something they do to make others feel comfortable.

❋ To keep dinner from becoming chaotic, don't allow siblings to interrupt one another. Use your authority as a parent to guide the conversations, not allowing one person to monopolize or another to get carried away with story antics. Do draw in those in your family who tend toward the quiet side.

❋ Just before everyone is finished eating, introduce your Table-Talk Christmas question. A parent should go first to model an appropriate answer.

❋ Resist the temptation to guide answers by saying things like, "That's not really your answer. Think harder." Each person should feel free to express his or her thoughts. Be encouraging. Remember, the goal isn't right and wrong, but communication. Be a good listener.

❋ When you feel it's appropriate, close with a brief prayer, or let one of your children pray.

✳ Let your family know what a pleasure it was having dinner with them. Be sure not to use dinner as a time for scolding about grades, chores, or other matters. If you make dinner simply a time to enjoy being together, you will find your family asking when you will be having dinner together again.

Making Table-Talk questions:

✳ If you have older children, set a Christmas basket or bag in the middle of the kitchen table, along with a pen and enough index cards for each person in your family. Once each week, instruct everyone in your family to think of a question, write it on a card, and place it in the basket. Choose one question to ask during each meal.

✳ If you have younger children, help them write it down separately so that their question will be a surprise to others.

$20 Treasure Hunt

Kim's Checking Out

J was finally ready for Christmas. I had put the last tag on the last package for the last person on my list. As I gathered up all the wrappings to put them away for another year, I felt that a magnificent weight had been lifted from my shoulders. I couldn't wait to curl up on the living room sofa and admire my twinkling tree, accented by a complete collection of gifts. As I sat sipping tea and patting myself on the back for having finished the shopping before Christmas Eve, my oldest son began sifting through packages.

Chase casually asked, "What did I get Bailey and Hannah?"

I knew it was too good to be true. I had forgotten to choose gifts for our kids to give each other. Every year I bought those gifts, too, and the kids just added their names to the tags. It always seemed the simplest way to include them. After years of my being the family's personal shopper, they didn't even expect to participate. Looking into the face of my 10 year old who was content to let me do his giving, I realized then that I had taken the easy way out and in the process had taught my children nothing about being a generous giver.

So the next day, my husband announced to the children that they would each receive an extra $20 with their regular allowance. With it they were to personally select family Christmas gifts. The kids couldn't wait to get started, and I was relieved not to have to think of one more perfect gift. So we loaded up the whole family and drove to a local discount store to seek out treasures that fit their $20 budgets.

My oldest son was the first to make a choice. He found a Nerf ball for himself. He also spied some golf clubs and a new baseball glove he thought Santa might like to get him. The whole "buying for others" concept was new to him, so I reviewed the main principle. Once he was back on track I went to help his younger brother.

Struggling with where to start, I pointed out two gifts Bailey could give his dad. He liked them both but couldn't decide. When I told him how much of his Christmas money each would cost, he looked shocked. "My money?" he questioned. "Aren't you paying for it?" Again, I explained to him the reason he received the extra $20 with his allowance. "But Dad said that was because it was Christmas," he said. After a lengthy discussion, he finally understood and chose the less expensive gift, getting his first economics lesson—$20 doesn't go far.

There was no misunderstanding on the part of our six-year-old daughter. She remembered that I was about to buy myself an overnight bag at that very store, and she insisted that I wait because "someone" might buy it for me. Then, worried that she had given away the surprise, she asked me what else I might like. Since the overnight bag would have cost the whole $20, I was eager to show her other options. I pointed out a decorative bowl for just $1.49 and a picture frame that was $2.50.

She slipped away with her dad, ducking through aisles hoping not to be seen as she made her secret purchases. We met up at the entrance where she stood with her fist full of change. "Dad is putting my presents in the car. You'll never guess what I got you," she boasted. "We're going to another store to buy the boys' presents."

They arrived home later, still whispering secrets, and locked themselves in a room to wrap gifts. "I got you something, Mom," Hannah announced. "But don't come in. I don't want you to know what it is." I didn't see her again until she walked to the tree carrying a bowl-shaped gift. "You'll never guess what I got you," she said confidently. Then she reappeared carrying a luggage-shaped gift.

She had spent all $20, plus two months of her allowance buying gifts for the rest of us, carefully wrapping each one to "hide" the contents. She was practically beside herself with anticipation of the moment we would unwrap her packages and get our surprises.

The boys also finished their shopping, although they didn't see the need to spend more than the original $20. Still, once they got started, they made a serious effort to choose gifts they thought the others would enjoy. Chase decided to give the Nerf football to his dad so they could play in the backyard together. He gave me potholders. "That way you won't burn your hands when you make my favorite foods," he informed me. From Bailey I received a stuffed blue coyote to stand guard on my nightstand. I think Dad got tools.

They put the most effort into choosing gifts for one another. I was surprised at how well each one knew the other's interests. When those gifts were opened Christmas morning, each one of my children beamed with pride. They could hardly wait to explain why their gift was just perfect for the other person. What a change from the years before.

First, it gave us a great family night. We laughed and enjoyed sneaking through aisles so that no one saw the gifts they were getting. It was a fun evening focused on our family. But it also gave our kids an opportunity to think about pleasing someone else. On this one night they were able to put every person in our family ahead of themselves. When they did, they found that it brought them satisfaction to be a giver. The $20 Treasure Hunt has become one of our favorite traditions.

TIPS FOR YOUR TREASURE HUNT

✳ This outing teaches some valuable lessons, but it doesn't have to cost an arm and a leg. Be sure to shop at a store that has discounted prices so that your children's money will go further.

✳ Remind your children a month ahead of time that the Treasure Hunt is coming. If they want to set aside some allowance or do extra chores to earn Christmas money, they will have plenty of time to save. They can add this to the budget you give them.

✳ Don't discourage your kids from the gift that they want to choose. That is the whole point. If they ask for your help, of course advise them, but let them make the decision so that the gift is really from them—even if you wind up with a blue coyote.

✳ You may want to consider a family devotional before the shopping trip. Some ideas that would be appropriate are teaching about God's gift of the Holy Spirit, looking to the interests of others, or Jesus as the best gift that was ever given.

✳ If you are a blended family and your children will need to shop for another parent or family, you can always plan a special trip just for that purpose. Helping him or her focus on the parent who is away will be a gift to your child.

TREE-RIFIC HOLIDAY FAMILY NIGHTS

Pam's Tree Traumas

*a*s a child we set aside December 2, my mom's birthday, for tree day. This wasn't some celebration of the environment, but the day we put up the Christmas tree, hung lights, and strung ornaments. The day included listening to music on the antique Victrola, drinking hot chocolate or eggnog, and bringing out all the Christmas boxes. As we opened each one, we reminisced about the origin of every ornament.

When I grew up and got married, I expected our first Christmas as a couple to center on that beloved childhood tradition. Unfortunately, when Jerry and I were married our ministry schedule ruled out even having a tree. Our staff positions with Campus Crusade for Christ had us traveling the whole season. So for years tree day was just a memory.

It wasn't until our first baby was due that we spent Christmas at home. Since I was eight months pregnant with Madison, I was unable to travel. We would be hosting Christmas for my parents and my sister's family for a change. That meant I would finally get that long-awaited tree.

Though I desperately wanted to help choose our very first tree, early contractions left me confined to home. The responsibility then fell to my husband to choose the tree I had dreamed about for so many years.

He left the house, assuring me he would purchase the best tree available. An hour later he returned giddy with excitement. How Jerry managed to lift that tree alone, I still wonder. It was enormous. When he finally got the tree in the stand and stood it up in our little rental house, the living room was dwarfed. The tree dominated the entire space, bending as it collided with the ceiling. It was not the tree of my dreams.

Three years later, we bought our first home. I was excited to think that I finally had a living room large enough to hold any tree Jerry could find. When Christmas came, Jerry and Madison set off on another tree adventure. I stayed home re-arranging the furniture in anticipation of a Goliath tree.

They were gone for hours. I envisioned the trouble they were having placing the largest tree on the farm in our mini-van. But I was prepared for anything—at least I thought I was. In they came beaming, carrying not a Goliath tree, but a Charlie Brown Christmas tree. Jerry explained that three-year-old Madison had fallen in love with the scraggliest and smallest. "It's just my size," she said. After giving that look only a daughter could give a daddy, he caved and she got her heart's desire. I made a mental note that nothing would keep me from joining the hunt the next year. And nothing did.

As I led the adventure the next Christmas, I found the perfect place to tree shop—Wal-Mart. In minutes we agreed upon a beautiful noble fir. It appeared that all the problems of the past were behind us. This tree was truly the right size.

Sadly, we discovered when we got home that it was not the right shape. The trunk had an awkward bow to it that required some effort to balance it in the stand. The kids and I painted ornaments while Jerry hung the Christmas lights on the branches. Then we opened their special ornament boxes and let them hang their treasures. All the while, Christmas music was playing as we sipped on cider and munched on cookies. It was the Tree Night I had always dreamed of having. I went to bed satisfied that finally Christmas was in hand.

We awoke the next morning to Madison's shrieks. She got up early to find that our specially decorated tree had crashed on its side. It was salvageable, but many homemade ornaments were shattered. Jerry went to work righting the tree. He assured me the problem was fixed. The tree fell a total of four more times. In the process of securing it, we nailed it to the wall, anchored it with cinder blocks, and had a maze of wire throughout the living room. Does it surprise you that we now celebrate with an artificial tree?

It took me a while to learn that the kind of tree doesn't really matter. The joy of a special day is in being together, not in having the perfect tree. With that focus, setting aside a special night for your family's unique decorating traditions will be something that your children will want to repeat for years to come.

Below are some tips for a successful family night built around tree decorating. Everyone's Tree Night will look different, but creating such a night is a sure formula for family togetherness, memories that last, and a family that is set apart.

TIPS FOR TREE-RIFIC FAMILY NIGHTS

Tree hunting and tree decorating are two separate family-night traditions for us since both require time and planning.

When going on a tree hunt:

※ Before going on your family hunt, get the tree stand out of storage and ready for use. Put out a bucket of water to soak the tree trunk when you bring it home. Taking care of these details ahead of time will keep the fun moving.

❋ Discuss with your family the tree-hunting options. You may want to do something different each year, or your family may always choose the same adventure.

❋ Many communities have a Christmas-tree farm within a reasonable distance. Choose an afternoon when everyone in your family can participate. Dress warm, take a thermos of hot chocolate or cider, and play Christmas music on the way. When you arrive, many places will give you a saw and allow you to cut down your tree. Be sure to take a video camera or a regular camera to record the moment. Let everyone participate in choosing the tree. Narrow your choice to two or three and take a vote on the winning tree. After you decide, let each person have a turn to saw on the tree and have his or her picture taken. Take a family picture when you load it on the car.

❋ Another option is to visit a local tree lot or a discount center's tree lot. Since the car ride will probably be short, stop by a café for drinks or dessert, or make a detour to see neighborhood Christmas lights. You will want to have your camera ready at these places, too. (No matter where you buy your tree, take something special to leave with the salesman. For ideas, see the chapter called Gift with Purchase in the "Season Your Surroundings" section.)

❋ When you get home with a live tree, saw off a few inches of the trunk and put your tree in the bucket of water you prepared.

❋ If you use an artificial tree, make unpacking it a special event. Sip eggnog or hot chocolate. Play Christmas music. Let everyone help assemble the branches.

❋ When your fresh tree is soaking or your artificial tree is assembled, join hands around the tree and sing a favorite carol, like "O Christmas Tree." Then briefly talk about when you will be decorating the tree. Anticipation is good, but young children have a hard time waiting, so plan to have your decorating night the next evening if possible.

Pray as a family for a Christmas season focused on celebrating God's gift to us—Jesus.

When planning Tree-Decorating Night:

Tree-Decorating Night will be more enjoyable if you take care of some preliminary tasks before calling your family together.

- ❄ Hang the lights on the tree ahead of time since strands may have to be untangled and bulbs replaced. Done ahead of time, it keeps children from becoming impatient.
- ❄ Plan to have all of your ornaments set out and ready to hang. If your children have individual ornament boxes, set those by the tree as well.
- ❄ Gather all the supplies you will need: tinsel, hooks, snow, tree skirt, or any other special items. Now's a good time to load the CD player with Christmas music.
- ❄ Inspect your tree topper in advance to ensure that it is in good shape and that all the bulbs work. It's anticlimactic to plug in the star and find that it doesn't work.
- ❄ Prepare a special holiday snack or drink to serve as you decorate.
- ❄ When it is finally time to start your Tree-Decorating Night, unplug the phone so that you can give full attention to your family.
- ❄ Don't start too late. When children are tired, the mood can quickly be spoiled.

Ideas for a creative Tree-Decorating Night:

- ❄ Choose a fun and special way to announce the beginning of Tree-Decorating Night. You may march through the halls singing a holiday song that tells your family Tree-Decorating Night has begun. You may have a special bell you ring.

Make it so exciting even older children and teens won't want to miss it.

✻ As everyone gathers, you may want to repeat a special phrase like, "Hear ye, hear ye! It is hereby declared that the Smith Family Tree Night has begun. So grab a decoration and let's have some fun." Remember, traditions are things that set your particular family apart from all others. Be creative or even a little silly.

✻ Now is the time to relax and enjoy all your tedious preparation. Reminisce over ornaments in your collection. Talk about what each person is excited about during this holiday.

✻ Don't stress out about how little children hang ornaments. Your tree may seem a little bottom-heavy for the first few years, but when you look back, even that will be a fond memory.

✻ If an ornament gets broken, don't stress or be surprised. If you plan on it happening, it won't spoil the night when it does. Just sweep away the pieces and focus on having fun.

✻ Halfway through the decorating, serve the snacks you prepared ahead of time.

✻ Depending on your children's ages, attention spans will vary. Toddlers and teenagers will be the first to drop out. Don't be frustrated if they don't want to stick it out to the very last ornament. Be prepared to stop in a timely way.

✻ Plan to end as a family. Assign each person a special concluding task so that they all participate. One can put the angel on the top, another can hang the Christmas Nail—always the last ornament we put up (more about this later). When all the house lights have been turned off, another child gets to plug in the tree. We rotate these each year so that everyone gets to do the special jobs.

✻ The moment the tree lights up, give a big cheer as a family.

❄ Close your special time in prayer. Keep it short since everyone may be tired, but ask God to bless your family and ask Him to help you find ways to encourage others during the season of Jesus' birth.

Season Your Surroundings

*"Behold, the Lamb of God who takes away
the sin of the world!"*
—JOHN 1:29, NASB

GIFT WITH PURCHASE

Kim's Shop and Shine

*a*ccording to Solomon, there is a time for everything under the sun. A time to live, a time to die; a time to laugh, a time to cry; a time to search, and a time to give up as lost.

I wonder if he wrote those final words when he was searching for a Furby. It all started when I read a report just before Christmas listing that year's top-10 toys. The first nine we already had, but Furby was different. Furby could speak two languages (English and Furbish) and had a vocabulary of 200 words and 800 phrases. He could sing, dance, and even catch a cold—all for the bargain price of $29.95. It was the have-to-have Christmas present of 1998, and I just had to have one.

My search started by calling every retailer within 50 miles, asking for Furby. Responses ranging from laughs to grumbles always ended the same: "Try after Christmas." My only hope was to catch an area store just as it received a shipment. So I went from one store to another, day after day, only to be told, "We won't get any more before Christmas."

Discouraged, I came to the last store. "You probably don't," I said to the clerk, pessimism oozing with every word, "but do you have Furby?"

"This is your lucky day," said the cashier. "We're expecting a shipment this afternoon." She handed me one of the five remaining claim tickets. All I had to do was come back that evening with the ticket and Furby was mine. I couldn't believe my search was almost at an end. Twenty stores and two weeks of searching were finally going to pay off.

Hours later, I presented my ticket to a clerk. "I'm here to pick up a Furby," I announced.

"Oh . . . well . . ." she said anxiously with that deer-caught-in-the-headlights look. "It seems that box is missing. I mean, it could be in the back of the truck. We're just not sure. What I mean, is . . . I don't have your Furby." She backed up a few steps in anticipation of my reply.

Her nervousness seemed a little odd, but I pressed on. "Will they be unloading the truck tonight?" She nodded, but said she didn't know if the box was actually there.

"That's okay," I told her. "If not, I'll try back another day."

Relief registered on her face. "Thank goodness." She shuddered. "I've been yelled at by several people in the last half hour because they have a claim ticket and I don't have their Furby."

Finally, I understood all the fearful and anxious faces I'd been seeing behind the counters. Day after day, clerks had been confronted by joyless, frustrated shoppers angered by inconveniences. On that day, I was thankful I had not been one of them. But what about the day before? I could vividly recall my frustration at having to wait in long lines, my curtness because I was running late, and my less-than-pleasant demeanor after a long day of shopping. With every purchase I made, I was at best indifferent, at worst . . . well, I'm sure you have your own stories. Suffice it to say, I had missed many opportunities to be a light in someone else's dark day.

That episode prompted our family's Gift-with-Purchase program. At the beginning of the holiday we fill a basket with ornaments that we have made on a family night. Everything in the basket is representative of some part of the Christmas story. We make angels, stars of Bethlehem, and crowns. On each one we attach a Bible verse that conveys the true meaning of Christmas. From Thanksgiving until Christmas Eve, we keep this basket of ornaments in the car. Whenever we go into a store, a restaurant, or even the dry cleaners, we take one of these ornaments to give to the person who assists us.

We have found that giving a gift with our purchase does two things. First, it helps keep us accountable for our attitudes around others. We can't very well gripe someone out for giving us the wrong change and then offer him or her a spiritually significant gift. Even greater, though, is what happens in the attitude of the people who receive it. In a small way it says that they are valuable, what they do is important, and they are appreciated. We will never know what effect the Word of God has in the life of each stranger as he or she reads the verse attached to the ornament, but we are happy to leave that responsibility with God. For our part, the blessing comes back when a smile crosses the face of someone who received our Gift with Purchase.

By the way, I eventually did secure a Furby. When my son opened it Christmas Eve, he took one look and said, "What is it?" Apparently, he had not read the top-10 list.

TIPS FOR PREPARING YOUR GIFT WITH PURCHASE
❋ Filling the basket full of give-away ornaments that you will keep in your car makes a great family night activity. Be sure to prepare all the supplies ahead of time so that kids don't get restless waiting. If you have very young children, you may want to have most of the ornaments assembled, with finishing touches left for them to do.
❋ Choose an ornament design that is simple to make and durable enough to keep in the car. Our favorite is the

coffee-filter angel. Instructions for this ornament are included. If you prefer to use a different craft idea, just be sure it has a symbolic Christian meaning.

✻ As your children work, talk to them about the command Jesus gave us to be the light of the world (Matthew 5:14). Keep the Bible open nearby to look up this and other verses.

✻ Don't forget to attach an appropriate Bible verse to each ornament. Remind your children that Scripture has an eternal power of its own, and God says it will not go out without accomplishing His purposes.

✻ When all the ornaments are completed, lead a family prayer time. Ask God to help the people who receive the ornaments understand more about Jesus' purpose on this earth and what makes Christmas such a holy holiday. Allow your children to pray if they want to.

GIFT-WITH-PURCHASE GIVE-AWAY IDEA

Making an angel:

For each angel you will need:

4 large coffee filters

12-inch piece of ribbon

4 inches of a gold pipe cleaner

glue gun

glue sticks

1. To make the head of the angel, crumple a coffee filter up into a ball. Lay it in the center of a fresh coffee filter and fold it in half. Scrunch the filter together and tie a small ribbon at the base of the ball to form a head, leaving an angel robe hanging down.

2. Fold another coffee filter in half and hot glue it to the back of the base of the head. This will add a second layer to the angel's robe.

3. Gather another coffee filter in the middle creating two wings. Hot glue this to the same spot at the back of the head.

4. Bend a pipe cleaner into a halo with a stem and glue the stem over the wings.

5. Attach this (or another) Bible verse to the ribbon: "Behold, I bring you good news of a great joy which shall be for all the people; for today in the city of David there has been born for you a Savior, who is Christ the LORD" (Luke 2:10-11, NASB).

IT'S A WRAP

Kim's Comfort Pie

being the baby sister, I have never been expected to take a big role in holiday preparations. My mom still cooks the feast, my sister usually helps, and I just mill around the kitchen licking bowls. This strategy worked for me even into my thirties. However, when my daughter, Hannah, asked why we never brought anything to the family dinners as her Aunt Tammi did, I realized the time had come to grow up. I determined to make at least one dish to contribute to our holiday feast. I would make a dessert.

When I conferred with six-year-old Hannah, she quickly volunteered to help. We both agreed that a few test runs would be in order before choosing the debut dessert. The first experiment would be a chocolate chess pie. Hannah suggested that we should use the freshest ingredients. Only handpicked and shelled pecans would be good enough. Luckily, she knew just where to find them. We were off to the city park.

Hannah and I ate a picnic lunch and began to plot a strategy for pecan picking. There were too many trees to search under every one, so we chose based on traffic patterns. Trees that were close to the trails had probably already been picked over thoroughly. Those in the back of the grove were the obvious choice, so we didn't go there. That's the first place a novice would hunt. We started under the trees near the public bath-rooms. We were sure to find plenty, as the flies would keep all but the serious pecan hunters away.

At first we searched side by side. I pointed out pecans and she bent over to pick them up. (I was saving my strength for baking.) We made a great team. After a while, though, we didn't agree on the search method. So we split up. We soon met again along the trail and pooled our resources. Together we had enough pecans for three pies.

A bystander seemed quite impressed with our take and stopped to praise our success. He was an older gentleman, in his seventies. "You young ladies having any luck?" he asked.

"Yes, sir," Hannah answered. "We have enough to make three pies." He was impressed with our accomplishment since he had only been able to find a dozen pecans himself.

"Yeah," he said as if we had asked him a question. "I like to come out here. People ask me what I do to keep busy. Well, I lost my wife 17 years ago and I just can't sit inside those four walls day after day. It is just too lonely. So I come out here sometimes. I just can't stay in those four walls day after day, alone." And then he shuffled off, alone.

My heart ached for that kind old man. I thought about him in the house where he raised his kids, celebrated anniversaries with his wife, and now sat alone not making memories, just reliving them. My daughter and I stopped picking pecans to ask God to send him comfort and companionship. Then a voice echoed in my mind, "I did. And you just let him walk away alone."

As the old man drove away in his little red pickup, I thought of the times I have despaired and felt alone. Who did God send my way? How many times did He show me His grace and mercy through the words of someone else? What impor-tant things did others set aside to be a comfort to me?

I recalled a familiar Bible passage: "Praise be to the God and Father of our Lord Jesus Christ, the Father of compassion and the God of all comfort, who comforts us in all our troubles, so that we can comfort those in any trouble with the comfort we ourselves have received from God" (2 Corinthians 1:3-4).

I went back to the park the next day hoping for another opportunity to pass on the compassion that I had received so many times before. The lonely man wasn't there. He must have stayed home inside those four walls. I had missed my opportunity and instead got caught just licking the bowl of God's goodness rather than offering to share it with someone else.

That encounter taught me that it was time to grow up in God's grace toward others. As I did, I could also teach my children the importance of giving themselves as gifts. We couldn't go back and be a blessing to the man in the park, but there were plenty of others we could reach out to with kindness. As a family, we were committed to a new task, reaching out to our older friends and wrapping them in love.

One way we do that is with Wrap-It-Up Night. Each year we send a letter to elderly friends and neighbors offering to come to their homes to wrap presents and help them with other holiday preparations. It is the best gift we give all year. And for those who receive it, it's more than a helping hand. It is an evening of friendship and laughter and the joy of being remembered. Even during the busy holiday, you will find that there is time to wrap a friend in love.

TIPS FOR YOUR WRAP-IT-UP NIGHT

❋ Send out your Wrap-It-Up announcement two weeks before you want to visit. Let the recipients know that you will call to set up a time to help.

❋ Ask them how they would like you to help. That will determine what you need to take with you.

❋ If they need help decorating, be sure to carry a step stool, a hammer, small nails, and other supplies that you may need.

❋ If your family is going to wrap gifts, ask if they already have wrapping paper, or if they would like you to shop for that for them. Take tape and enough scissors for everyone in your family to help. If you have young children, they can put on tags and bows and carry the gifts to the tree.

❋ If your friends need baking done, be sure to ask what ingredients are needed. You may need to stop at the store for them.

❋ If they need help cleaning before company arrives, ask about supplies.

❋ Take along a portable CD player and some Christmas music.

❋ Pack some envelopes of hot chocolate or powdered apple cider.

❋ Be sure to spend some time just visiting with the person or couple. Your companionship will be the greatest gift of all.

❋ Make your children an essential part of the evening of giving. It will set an example of compassion that will last a lifetime.

Let us help you get Christmas wrapped up

Our family would like to make an appointment to come to your house and help with your holiday chores. We can:

Wrap gifts
Decorate trees
Hang lights
Bake goodies

It's our Christmas gift to you!

We will call you to find a time when we can get together.

SWEET REMEMBRANCES
Kim's First Good-byes

We love to commemorate firsts—first step, first tooth, first home run, and first date. Even first broken bones have been marked at our house by special recognition. That honor went to my middle son, Bailey, who fractured a growth plate in his arm while attempting a back flip on the trampoline. It was a painful experience that ended with a sling for his friends to sign. Fortunately, time and a few visits to the doctor's office were all it took to heal that wound. I'm happy to report that he is growing normally and has moved on to bigger and better firsts, like being the first to drop the cat down the laundry chute, first to be in a musical, and first to hold a tarantula. Those are just a few in a long list of firsts our family has had the fun of commemorating.

Not all firsts, however, are the kind you feel like celebrating. Some are the kind that must be endured, like the first time you lose a loved one. The year 2000 was like that for both my husband and me. Within four months, June to September, his mother and my stepfather both died unexpectedly. It was the first time we had lost a parent and the first time the kids had to say good-bye to a grandparent. For his stepdad and my mom, it was just the beginning of a long road of firsts without their beloved partners.

As the holidays approached, we all wondered what Thanksgiving and Christmas would be like without Grandma Tera and Grandpa Cliff. It had been months since we said good-bye, but the grieving came fresh at unexpected times. It was painful to remember but unbearable to forget. Facing the holidays for us seemed a long and lonely journey—a journey that others could not take with us.

Then one day I opened my mailbox to find a card from a woman who was really no more than an acquaintance. She had lost her father two years before and wrote that she knew we would be facing difficult days as Christmas approached. Since she had had the opportunity to meet my dad, she took the time to reflect on his pleasant manner and quick sense of humor and to say he was indeed missed. She concluded by assuring me that my family was in her prayers, particularly my mother. Then she added a postscript with this verse:

> "But we do not want you to be uninformed, brethren, about those who are asleep, that you may not grieve as do the rest who have no hope. For if we believe that Jesus died and rose again, even so God will bring with Him those who have fallen asleep in Jesus. . . . For the LORD Himself will descend from heaven with a shout, with the voice of the archangel and with the trumpet of God, and the dead in Christ will rise first. Then we who are alive and remain shall be caught up together with them in the clouds to meet the LORD in the air, and so we shall always be with the LORD. Therefore comfort one another with these words" (1 Thessalonians 4:13-18, NASB).

Those words were comforting and came at a time when the weight of the grief was heavy. It was a sweet remembrance given by a woman I hardly knew but who took the time to bear some of my burden. It was truly a balm for my spirit.

My husband received the same sort of encouragement on the first anniversary of his mother's death. A package arrived on June 8, an ordinary day to most of the world, but a watershed of memories for Tony. After opening the box, he found a framed black-and-white photograph of himself, his brother, his stepdad, and his mother. The note with it read, "Tony, I came across this picture the other day and thought you would like to have it. I think of your mom often. She was so good to us. We really miss her. We are praying for you." The note and picture were from his cousin Tracey, a young woman just out of college. It meant so much to Tony that someone else was still thinking about his mother, remembering and missing her. In a way it validated the loss that he still felt on that difficult "first" and comforted him at the same time.

Of all the firsts that we endure when someone we love leaves us, it is first anniversaries and holidays that are the hardest. Is someone you know experiencing a first this Christmas? You and your family can season your surroundings with comfort and encouragement by reaching out with sweet remembrances. Below is a list of ideas to consider. Talk with your family about other ways to bring support to specific people who need it. Remember, this is not something you can do just for a close friend or family member. Reach out to neighbors, church members, and even casual acquaintances who you know are facing a difficult time of transition. If you haven't already overloaded your holiday plate, consider a sweet remembrance.

IDEAS TO SEASON WITH COMFORT

* First and foremost, don't be afraid to mention the person they have lost. Nothing is worse than thinking that everyone has forgotten the person you loved and miss.
* Mail them an encouraging card.
* Mention specific memories that you have of that person.

❊ Include scriptures that are appropriate in his or her situation.

❊ Invite him or her to lunch or coffee and be a good listener. Some great questions are "How are you really doing?" and "What are you struggling with most?" So many people avoid the subject of grief you may find your friend is longing to talk with someone about what he or she is going through.

❊ Send a note to children who have lost their grandparents. A particularly good time would be when they have accomplished something their grandparent would have enjoyed seeing. Remind them how proud their grandparent was of them.

❊ Put a grieving person's name or picture on the refrigerator and pray for him or her at family mealtimes during the holidays.

❊ Make a donation to a cause that your friend's loved one cared about, then send a note to say it was done in memory of that person.

❊ Place flowers at the front of the church in the loved one's memory.

❊ Encourage other friends to drop notes in the mail throughout the Christmas season.

Scriptures that are appropriate concerning hope, peace, and comfort:

❊ Our future hope: Psalm 49:15; Proverbs 14:32; Isaiah 25:8; John 11:25-26; 1 Corinthians 15:55; Romans 8:38-39; 1 Thessalonians 4:13-18

❊ God's peace: Psalm 32:7, 18:28; Isaiah 40:2; John 14:2, 16:33; Philippians 4:7

❊ God's comfort: Psalm 18:2, 27:14, 55:22; Matthew 11:28; 2 Corinthians 1:5

OPPORTUNITY KNOCKING

Cross Country with Pam

*W*e have been privileged to participate in some incredible outreach experiences through our full-time Campus Crusade ministry to students.

When Madison was four years old, we were assigned to a summer beach outreach in Santa Cruz, California. We trained students to confidently tell others about the life of Christ and about Christ in their lives; then we sent them to the beach to share with others. As I trained girls how to briefly retell their own stories of meeting and receiving Christ, Madison sat with us, listening intently. After a while she interrupted to say, "Mommy, it's my turn. I wrote my testimony." We all gave her our undivided attention as she began. "When I was three and I was in my room, I asked Jesus to come into my life. Can I share that with someone?" I was reminded at that moment that what we were involved in wasn't just a great training ground for students; it was also a training ground for my children. They, too, were growing a heart for reaching the lost with every project we were assigned.

The trip that changed our lives the most was the summer we led a student project in another country. Though we went as a family, Jerry had many responsibilities that kept him busy, but the kids and I were busy too. We spent our days looking for opportunities to tell others about Jesus' life, a real challenge in a Middle Eastern country.

But where should we start? Time and time again the words of Dr. Bill Bright, the founder of Campus Crusade for Christ, came to my mind. Whenever he spends five minutes with someone, he sees that as "a divine opportunity from God" to tell that person about the Savior. That was the mindset I wanted to have, so I started looking for mini-encounters, and they came regularly.

Keeping Dr. Bright's words in mind, we reached out to taxi drivers, shoppers at the market, families, and strangers drawn to us because we spoke English. Every day we prayed that God would give Madison, Connor, and me big eyes to see and big ears to listen for the opportunities God would bring our way.

After we returned home there were so many things to do to get back to our old life. Mail had to be sorted, errands had to be run, and calls needed to be made. As we were going about these normal tasks, Dr. Bright's words came back to me again. "Five minutes with anyone is a divine opportunity." As I put on my big eyes and big ears, I realized that God was giving me just as many opportunities in my hometown to tell others about Jesus as He had when I was half a world away. God was teaching me that in His eyes, every encounter was an official assignment from Him no matter where we were.

Your family may not get the opportunity to travel 10,000 miles to share the gospel with the lost. Maybe you won't even travel coast-to-coast. But what about traveling to your neighbor's house across the street? Would you be willing to look for opportunities at your office, in the ladies club, at your children's schools, at the grocery store, the bank, and the deli? These are our divinely appointed mission fields, and they can be just as exciting as a spot around the globe. The mission is the same; tell others about Jesus Christ so that when they hear about Him, they too will have the opportunity to receive Him.

Life for a Christian is all about knowing God and taking the opportunity to tell others about Jesus' divine purpose. Christmas is one of those great opportunities. As we approach Christmas, the message of the Nativity should accompany the message of Christ's sacrifice at the cross and His glorious promise of eternal life. Jesus came to take away the sins of the people. This is the truth we can share during our divine holiday appointments. And we can do it in creative ways.

One way our family shares Jesus' story is through the Christmas Nail. The Christmas Nail is an eight-inch spike that represents the nails used to secure Jesus to the cross. A card is tied to the nail with a red ribbon. It reads: "This Christmas Nail is a secret ornament. Place it in the center of your tree so that only your family knows of its presence. Others will take no notice of it, but to you the nail symbolizes the tree that Jesus decorated for us with the sacrifice of His life." This verse is also on the card. "But God demonstrates His own love for us in this: While we were still sinners, Christ died for us" (Romans 5:8).

As a family, we make a basket of these Christmas Nails and set it by the front door. Whenever divine opportunity literally knocks on our door, we're ready with a creative way to share the real purpose of Jesus' birth. When the doorbell rings, my children run to see who will receive the nail they will personally deliver. It could be the UPS driver, the meter reader, the pizza delivery guy, or maybe a neighbor coming to borrow sugar.

For those neighbors who haven't had a reason to drop by, we visit them just before Christmas to give them our special gift. If this idea fits your family, just follow our tips to help you be ready when opportunity knocks.

Tips for making Christmas Nails

❋ At the hardware store ask for a box of eight-inch landscaping spikes.

❋ Purchase a spool of ¼-inch red ribbon from the fabric store. Cut in eight-inch pieces.

❋ On your computer, print the Christmas Nail message and verse, quoted above, onto card stock. The finished card, after cutting, should be about 3 by 5 inches. You can print four message cards on one 8½-by-11-inch sheet of card stock. Be creative. You will be able to find many seasonal graphics on your publishing software.

❋ If you do not have a computer, you can handwrite the message on an index card.

❋ Use a hole-punch to put a hole in the corner of the message card.

❋ Tie the ribbon onto the top of the nail and then tie the ribbon through the card.

❋ Place the nails in a sturdy basket by your front door.

❋ Give one to each of your children to put away in their ornament boxes for the future.

❋ Besides using them to give away at home, Christmas Nails are also good gifts for teachers, holiday party exchanges, church staff, and others who would treasure a reminder of Christ's sacrifice on the tree.

COFFEE AND CAROLING

Dinner for 80 at Kim's

*M*y mother is a master entertainer. She can think of more ways to set a table, serve a meal, and make guests feel special, all without losing her cool. Of course, her forte is preparing the perfect food for any occasion. She is a great cook. I've been told that I am just like my mother—except for the cooking and entertaining thing.

When I invite guests for dinner, they usually arrive while I'm taking the meat from the freezer. I can hardly wait for them to say those three little words all guests feel obliged to utter, "Can I help?" Immediately I put them to work chopping salad, setting the table, or flinging raw meat into a pan. They tend to be much better helpers than my children.

Though I lack the skills and temperament to be the kind of hostess my mother is, I sincerely desire to learn. I even make attempts to walk in her footsteps. Every year we invite about 80 people to a Christmas party in our home. It is the one time when I know that I can't wing it. Not only is cooking and entertaining an issue, but cleaning becomes an all-consuming task. Days ahead of time I start conquering all the piles that have been accumulating since the last Christmas party. But I don't stop there. What if someone were to look inside my linen closet or under my children's beds? Totally out of my nature I become obsessive-compulsive about uncluttering the nooks and crannies of my home. I clean everything from sock drawers to ceiling fans, just in case a crazed guest should go on a white-glove rampage.

Christmas party time is also the perfect incentive to get to that major house project we've been putting off. If I can just get into the messy stage, I know my husband will come along and complete the project just in time for the party. One year we repainted all the front rooms of the house and were pulling down masking tape and hanging pictures literally minutes before the first guest arrived.

Cleaning and remodeling, though, are only half the effort. No party would be a success without a smorgasbord of fabulous food. You may be wondering how I manage to pull that off at the same time I am nailing drywall in the bathroom. The answer is obvious: My mother does all the cooking for our Christmas party. She spends weeks ahead of time test-cooking new recipes and planning every detail of food presentation. She works tirelessly to offer only the most succulent fare.

All of her effort is no secret to our friends. Before actually accepting our invitation, many pointedly ask, "Will your mom be cooking again this year?" Affirmation usually brings an acceptance right on the spot, proving that it's not my exceptionally clean house that our friends look forward to but the new delights Mom has prepared for them. If I were to announce that I would be cooking instead of my mother, attendance would drop by half. But I don't mind. Truthfully, if she weren't cooking, I probably wouldn't come either.

I still have much to learn from my mother, but she has already taught me a more important lesson than cooking. She has taught me the difference between entertaining and showing hospitality. Entertaining involves outer trappings; hospitality involves the heart. Where entertaining is an event that requires resources, hospitality is an invitation to friendship. Anyone can entertain, only those who value others can show hospitality. My mother can do both. She excels at entertaining, but she does it with a heart of hospitality.

Romans 12:13 encourages us to "practice hospitality," the later word defined as "love for strangers." We are to "be hospitable to one another without complaint" (1 Peter 4:9, NASB) and "not neglect to show hospitality to strangers" (Hebrews 13:2, NASB). The result of combining this kind of love with unselfish generosity is a genuine interest that breaks down barriers. It is a disarming gesture of friendship that opens the door for deeper life-changing relationships. With the holidays just around the corner, opportunities abound to use our homes to reach out and show "love for strangers" and generosity without complaining.

Below are two ideas, complete with tips for success. One is an outreach to adults, the other to children. The Christmas Coffee allows you to invite neighbors into your home and begin to build relationships. The Kids' Caroling event will utilize your home to reach boys and girls in your neighborhood or from your children's circle of friends while providing them a fun holiday activity. Both require very little entertaining but a lot of hospitality. Remember, it is your heart that will make the difference in the lives of those who come, not the menu or the way in which your home is decorated. Keep your focus on them and you will enjoy hosting as much as they will enjoy coming.

These ideas do take more planning than some of the other outreach ideas. If you choose to be a holiday hostess, be sure that you have time for all the things involved. It won't be a joy if your schedule is already overloaded. If it is, but you like these ideas, pray and ask God to clear your schedule for next year. When He does, make plans to welcome strangers (known these days as neighbors) into your home. It is a sure way to season your surroundings with God's love.

TIPS FOR HOSTING A CHRISTMAS COFFEE

This hospitality event is designed to provide an opportunity to build relationships with neighbors. It is a casual social night that will include a brief time for you to share the significance of Christmas through a story about how God has changed your life. You can use this same pattern to reach out to coworkers, acquaintances from your community organizations, or parents of your children's friends.

How to organize:

❋ Begin by praying regularly about the timing and preparation, for your neighbors' receptivity to learning about Jesus, and for boldness and confidence as you tell your story. If you know other Christians in your neighborhood, invite them to pray and be part of the event with you.

❋ Choose a date and a time. Take into account your town's community calendar. Avoid scheduling your coffee on a night when a big event is planned. Also consider the makeup of your neighborhood. Young families will need to feed children and settle a baby-sitter before arriving. Also remember that calendars get full as Christmas draws near. Early December on a weeknight from 7:00 until 8:30 P.M. usually works well.

❋ Prepare an invitation to be mailed to each home in your neighborhood about 10 days in advance. Be sure your phone number is included so they can contact you with questions or leave the number with the sitter. Note on the invitation if it is an adults only event. It is a good idea to include an RSVP for regrets. That way, even if they are unable to attend, you will have the chance to have a conversation.

❊ Prepare a door hanger that can be left the day before the event as a last-minute reminder. Pray for each family by name as you address the invitations and hang out the door hangers.

❊ Don't ask your guests to bring anything to this first gathering. You don't want them to have any obstacles to attending. Treat them instead.

❊ Here is the revolutionary part: Don't stress out about what you will serve. If you like to bake, go for it. But bake all the desserts you plan to serve the day before so that you have time for other important things the day of the coffee. If, like me, the very idea of preparing something edible would keep you from hosting your neighbors, then serve prepared desserts. You can get them from a bakery or from the bakery department of a grocery store. Remember, guests are not coming for food but for a chance to meet new friends. Keep that goal in mind.

❊ Just before guests arrive on the night of the party, place single servings of the dessert onto holiday plates so that you will not be stuck at the serving table later in the night. Set out cups, glasses, silverware, and napkins.

❊ Prepare a basket of Christmas Nails to set by the door so you can give each guest one of the ornaments as they leave your home.

❊ Set out a basket of name tags. It will help others feel comfortable with people they have not met.

❊ Set out plenty of chairs. Arrange them in groupings instead of along walls.

❊ Prepare a hot drink, such as wassail or coffee, and a cold drink, such as iced tea or punch.

❅ Choose meaningful music to be played that night. Christmas hymns or carols playing quietly in the background will add much to your evening.

❅ Most important, think through the personal testimony you will share that night. Your goal is not to preach to your neighbors but to let them know a little about you personally and about why Christmas is meaningful to you.

Tips for preparing an effective personal testimony:

❅ Keep it short, no longer than three minutes.

❅ In this particular case, include a welcome to your guests. Tell them you are so glad to be sharing a part of this special holiday with them. Then tell why it is so special to you.

❅ Let them know that you were not always a Christian. Tell them something of your life before Christ. Then tell them what changed. Your story should describe when you first heard the gospel. Explain what you came to understand about Jesus' life, death, and resurrection, how you received Christ as your personal Savior, and the difference it has made in your life. Be sure not to paint an unrealistic picture of a perfect life, but do let them see your hope in Christ.

❅ Each person who hears your story should know the message of Jesus' power to change lives forever and how he or she can have the same experience you did.

❅ Relate your story to why that makes Christmas significant to your family.

❅ Show your guests the Christmas Nail and tell them that, as a token of friendship, you would like each person to take one home.

❅ Then pray to God, asking for a blessing on each neighbor and for every person to desire to understand more about Jesus Christ and the hope He offers.

At the event:

❅ Since everything has been done in advance, you can be available to greet and visit with your guests. Remember, the goal is hospitality, not entertaining. Focus on building relationships with your neighbors. Ask deeper questions in your conversations. Avoid too many questions about kids, the weather, or church attendance.

❅ Introduce neighbors to one another.

❅ About 30 minutes into the party, invite guests to get coffee and dessert.

❅ Keep things casual and unstructured so that the focus remains on getting acquainted.

❅ About 20 minutes before the party is to end, ask for your guests' attention and share your holiday thoughts and story.

❅ As they leave, give them the Christmas Nail as a gift and tell them how much you enjoyed getting to spend time with them.

❅ Continue your outreach by praying for your neighbors and building on the relationships that were started.

HOSTING A KIDS' CAROLING PARTY FOR THE NEEDY

This event focuses on two things: reaching out to those in physical need and reaching out to those in spiritual need. First, organize a group of young carolers who will sing to neighbors for donations of food for the local food pantry. You will also share a devotion or message with the children while they celebrate their success at your house. I have designed this sample for 8- to 12-year-olds, but it can be adapted for students from kindergarten to college.

Planning the event:

❅ If this is not specifically a neighborhood outreach, make out the invitation list with your children.

✳ Let them help you pray for the children on the list. Pray specifically for a schedule that would allow them to come, for protection, and for God to prepare the children's hearts and minds to understand and believe the Christmas message.

✳ Make invitations to send to children. It should include a description of the event, the time, the place, your phone number, and instructions to dress in warm clothing and bring a flashlight. Mail them 10 days in advance.

✳ Make flyers to give to neighbors informing them that carolers may stop by and asking them to contribute non-perishable food to your caroling food drive. Put the flyers on the doors one day in advance.

✳ Have plenty of hot drinks and snacks ready to be served after caroling.

✳ Have name tags available.

✳ Set out plastic grocery sacks for each person expected.

✳ Choose five or six familiar Christmas carols and have the printed words available.

✳ Prepare the devotion and have your Bible and any needed materials handy.

At the event:

✳ Upon arrival, have the children put on name tags and begin practicing the words to the carols while they wait for others to arrive.

✳ After everyone arrives, assign each child a buddy to stay with during the caroling.

✳ Give the crowd food sacks. Remind them to get their flashlights and music sheets.

✳ Pray as a group that God would allow your songs to be a blessing to those who hear them. Also remember in prayer the people who need the food you're gathering.

✳ Give any instructions, such as no crossing the street, no yelling, no running, etc.

✳ If possible, leave an adult to have drinks poured and snacks ready at a designated time.

✳ Have another adult follow along in a car to collect the food.

✳ At the first house, allow a child to knock and explain that your group is caroling for food for the needy and if they would like to contribute after you sing you are accepting canned or packaged goods.

✳ Sing three carols at each house, before accepting a food donation.

✳ At the end of the hour, return to your house. Allow the children time to enjoy their snack before the devotion, or settle them in an area where a spill would not be a disaster during the devotion.

✳ After each person is settled on the floor, thank the group for helping to reach others in need. Talk about the kinds of needs that a homeless person might have: food, shelter, medical help, schooling. Talk about how a person can get help to meet those needs: shelter, church, government, someone nice. Let the kids brainstorm and participate in this part of the devotion. Then tell them something like this: "You're saying that when people can't help themselves, they have to count on someone else to help them. Right? Well, that is exactly what God did for us on Christmas day. He looked down and saw that everyone in the whole world, even those who were not born yet, needed help. And He knew He was the only one who could help."

✳ Then begin your prepared, kid-friendly devotion that will cover the story of Jesus' birth, life, death, and resurrection. Keep it brief, but be very specific about our need as sinners to be forgiven. Explain in simple words that God planned for Jesus to forgive us; that's why we need Him. Be sure that the children know the message comes from the Bible by reading a few related verses.

- ❄ At the end, give the children an opportunity to ask God to help them. "You might realize that you have done things that are wrong, called sins, and they need to be forgiven. The Bible has shown us that's why Jesus came, to forgive sins. If you would like to ask Jesus to help you, you can do that by praying right now and asking Him to forgive your sins. I'm going to say a prayer that you can listen to and pray silently along with me."
- ❄ After praying say something like, "If any of you said that prayer, I would love for you to tell me. But even if you don't, be sure to tell your mom or dad that you prayed to ask Jesus to forgive your sins. They will want to share that very special decision with you."
- ❄ Close in prayer, thanking God that He helps us by providing food for us as well as being our Friend who forgives us.
- ❄ Finish with one last Christmas carol out on the front porch as you wait for parents.

When everyone leaves, ask your family to pray that those who heard the complete Christmas message will come back and ask more questions about Jesus and the Bible

TREASURING TEACHERS

Kim Wier's Weird Career

I am a stay-at-home mom. Some would build me up with the title Domestic Engineer, or perhaps Chief Executive Officer of Wier and Company, but I prefer to keep expectations low. After all, engineers don't get to take a nap after a hard afternoon at the office. And CEOs who stop in the middle of the day for a hot bubble bath would be fired without a pension. No, I prefer just the title "stay-at-home mom," which, by the way, is an oxymoron, since everyone knows we are really "stay-in-the-car moms."

I haven't always felt this way. All through high school and college I envisioned myself as the high-powered corporate type, focusing first and foremost on my career. I was going to change the world. So I pursued a degree in journalism and set my sights on the big time, that is, until a charming guy named Tony set his sights on me.

After our marriage, it no longer seemed feasible to pursue a career in journalism, at least not the hard-hitting kind that had been the center of my dreams. So I decided on the next best thing—teaching journalism. Just after my first son was born, I went back to school to add a teaching certificate to my degree.

In the mornings I went to classes and in the afternoons I worked part-time. Every morning was like a race as I rushed to find shoes, make breakfast, gather books, and beat the clock. Only occasionally did I forget to put Chase in the car before heading down the road to take him to my sister's house. Coming home was no better. My schedule put me in the driveway just 10 minutes before my husband. My routine was to fly into the house, put in a Barney video, stick a snack in Chase's hand, run though the house picking up the toys, put water on to boil (even if I didn't know what I would be cooking), and try to look like I had it all under control by the time Tony walked through the door. By eight o'clock, when my son went to bed, I was comatose.

By the end of the year, with teaching certificate in hand, it was clear I lacked the organizational skills to balance family, home, and career. For me, something had to give. When I found out I was pregnant with baby number two, it became an easy choice. I would apply myself, not to changing the world, but to changing diapers, sheets, and vacuum-cleaner bags. I would be a stay-at-home mom.

I never dreamed that 10 years later I would get a chance to see what I had given up. At that time, my three children ranged in age from 8 to 12, and all attended the same small Christian school. One day the principal, Mrs. Harris, called me when the school needed a long-term substitute teacher.

"We need someone to sub in the kindergarten class for two weeks," she said. "You'll have to be there promptly at 7:45."

As she spoke, I had flashbacks to my last attempt at juggling work and home. But now my children were older, and, of course, I was more capable. Besides, it was only for two weeks. So of course I said, "No problem."

On the very first morning, I had problems. The alarm didn't sound, the coffeepot overflowed, and when we finally got in the car, the fuel gauge was on empty. I was not going to be in the classroom promptly. Instead, I flew in 10 minutes late and was greeted by 12 five-year-olds being supervised by the principal.

After sufficient groveling and promises to do better, I was left alone with only a lesson plan and a cup of coffee for survival.

"Good morning class. I'm Mrs. Wier. I am going to be your teacher for the next few days. We are going to have a lot of fun together, so let's get started."

Before I could give the first assignment, hands started going up all over the room.

"Mrs. Weird, can I sharpen my pencil?"

"Yes you may, but my name is Mrs. Wier."

Another hand. "Mrs. Weird, my puppy has worms and they come out his—"

"That's just terrible," I quickly interrupted. "But my name is Mrs. Wier."

Still, on and on it went, "Mrs. Weird" this and "Mrs. Weird" that. They could not say my name without tagging on that dreaded D—and they said it often. No matter how clearly I gave an instruction, at least half the hands went up to ask me what to do next.

It took three cups of coffee to get me through that first day, and when I got home, I was exhausted. Yet I still had a list of household chores to do, homework to supervise, dinner to cook, and pumpkins to cut out of construction paper for the next day's introduction to the letter *P*.

I managed to keep up for about three days. On the fourth day, I crashed. My husband came home from work and found the house a wreck and me sound asleep on the bed. When he asked the kids what was wrong with Mom, they gave him the same reply I had given them when they wanted their afternoon snack: "Mom said she has already put in her eight hours today. She's 'off duty.'"

That night, we all agreed on two things. First, I was not prepared to be a working mom. Second, our teachers deserve a great deal more appreciation than we give them.

Ninety percent of our children's teachers have a family that depends on them. When they finish their day at four or five o'clock, their work is not over. They are simply moving to the second shift as they go home to take on family responsibilities. Though it's the same story for all working moms what is different about teachers is the enormously significant role they play in not only their children's lives, but our children's as well. Under normal circumstances, they carry burdensome responsibilities. Add to that all of the extra duties that the holidays bring, and it is easy to have empathy for your child's teacher.

What better time than Christmas to show God's mercy and loving-kindness to a teacher you know. What a blessing it will be when we creatively provide encouragement to a teacher even as we seek to share the meaning behind Christ's birth.

Ways to Treasure a Teacher

❋ Make a teacher's holiday survival kit. Start with a seasonal gift bag that will hold the following: a package of gift tags, a magnetic to-do list and a fun pen, a small holiday-scented votive candle, three quick-and-easy casserole recipes handwritten on index cards, something chocolate, a homemade coupon for two hours of your help for grading or filing during the month of December, and a Christmas Nail. Be creative and add other things that would be helpful during the holiday rush. Print or hand write a survival kit tag to hang on the outside of the bag. Ours says:

Holiday Survival Kit
"May God supply all your needs
according to His riches in glory.

And may this little bag be helpful
as you focus on His story." The Wiers

❋ Make a casserole and write the teacher a card that tells her
you understand that she is pulling double duty by caring
for your child and then going home to care for her own.
Deliver the casserole when you pick up your child, or take
it frozen in the morning so that it will stay fresh. Add a
verse of encouragement or the text of the Christmas story
from Luke 2.

❋ Make a batch of cookies that she can take home to her
family. Let her know that you understand the sacrifices she
makes at home to be a good teacher for your child every
day. Add a verse of encouragement, perhaps Jesus' words
about children from Matthew 19:14: "Let the little children
come to me, and do not hinder them, for the kingdom of
heaven belongs to such as these."

❋ When choosing a teacher gift, to be given from either the
class or from your child, use the opportunity to give something spiritually significant. There are many appropriate
devotional books that would be an encouragement. Be sure
to inscribe it with words of appreciation.

❋ Provide your teacher with a list of resources that will help
him or her creatively present the biblical Christmas story
in the classroom. For example, the facts of Christ's birth
can legally be presented in the context of a geography lesson. It can also be discussed from a literary perspective or
as the teacher presents how cultures from around the
world celebrate Christmas. Without being pushy, you can
provide valuable tools that your teacher may enjoy present-
ing but lacks the time to prepare. Print off such ideas from
the Internet or other reliable sources.

❋ My favorite teacher gift is what we call the "Jesus Was a
Teacher Too" frame. It is simple to make if you have a

word processor program. All that is required is typing out the text of the Beatitudes from Matthew 5. If you want to embellish it, use a desktop publishing program such as Print Shop or Microsoft Publisher. Be creative or make it simple; the words are what will touch her heart. After you have printed out the text in an appropriate font, copy it on specialty parchment paper, trim it, and put it in an 8-by-10 frame that she would be proud to put on her desk or a shelf at home. We have included the one we give if you would like to copy it word for word.

Jesus Was a Teacher Too

*He opened His mouth
and began to teach them, saying,*

*"Blessed are the poor in spirit, for theirs is the kingdom of heaven.
Blessed are those who mourn, for they shall be comforted.
Blessed are the gentle, for they shall inherit the earth.
Blessed are those who hunger and thirst for righteousness,
for they shall be satisfied.
Blessed are the merciful, for they shall receive mercy.
Blessed are the pure in heart, for they shall see God.
Blessed are the peacemakers, for they shall be called sons of God."*

*When Jesus had finished these words,
the crowds were amazed at His teaching.*
—Matthew 5:2-9; 7:28, NASB

Savor Your Savior

You are worthy, our Lord and God,
to receive glory and honor and power,
for you created all things.
—REVELATION 4:11

ATTRIBUTE ORNAMENTS

Kim's Divine Decorating

*W*hen my son Chase was about five years old, he sat in church with us one Sunday morning flipping furiously through the pages of his Bible. After a few minutes I leaned over to asked what he was searching for.

"I can't find it," he said.

"You can't find what?" I asked.

"You know, that chapter in the Bible where God created everything. The Sega Genesis chapter."

I can see how he might have gotten the Bible confused with a video game. After all, much of what originated as sacred has taken on completely different meanings in the twenty-first century. A "righteous dude" is not necessarily a good man. "Holy cow" isn't referring to a sacrificial animal. And these days "angels" work for networks instead of God. In today's culture, few hallmarks of the faith remain untainted. But even if that were not so, kids have a limited frame of reference. They can easily misunderstand concepts and words that we consider a common part of our spiritual experience.

Chase came to us one day very concerned because he had heard something at church that didn't make sense. "Mom, didn't you say that God is all-powerful, that He can do anything?"

"That's right. He is all-powerful," I assured him.

"Then how come everybody at church is always singing about how tired He is?"

"Chase, what are you talking about?" I questioned.

"At church everybody sings, 'He is exhausted, the king is exhausted.' Why is He so exhausted if He has all that power?"

He couldn't assimilate the word "exalted" because he had never been exposed to it. So instead of understanding that God is praised above the entire universe, he thought God got worn out like his mom and dad. Those kinds of misunderstandings are a normal part of growing up. But just like we teach our child to hold a fork, to count to 10, and to write his name, we can also teach him fundamentals about God's nature. A fun way to do that is with Attribute Ornaments.

All you need are 25 glass Christmas balls, a paint pen, and a Bible. On each of the balls, write one attribute (or godly quality) of Jesus. When they are dry, place all the ornaments in a basket or a glass bowl beside the tree. Then each night of advent, choose one ball to add to the tree. Before you hang it on a limb, talk about ways that Jesus displayed that quality. Look up Bible verses that talk about them. Then pray together, praising God for that aspect of His character.

Once you have worked your way through all His attributes, you can make Namesake Ornaments another year, featuring all the different names of God the Father, God the Son, and God the Holy Spirit.

Knowing Jesus as the baby in the manger is a wonderful place to begin. It was His life as the God-Man, however, that fully revealed His divine nature. Exposing your children to the attributes of Jesus will lay a foundation for them that will help them to savor their Savior for a lifetime, not just during the holidays.

ATTRIBUTES OF JESUS

1. Faithful: 1 Corinthians 1:9, 4:17; 2 Thessalonians 3:3
2. Righteous: 1 John 2:1, 2:29
3. Holy: 1 Peter 1:15
4. Forgiving: Psalm 86:5; Colossians 3:13
5. Loving: Romans 8:35-39; Ephesians 2:4-5; Revelation 1:5
6. Merciful: Titus 3:5; James 5:11
7. All-Knowing (Omniscient): John 1:48
8. All-Present (Omnipresent): Psalm 139:7-12; Matthew 18:20
9. All-Powerful (Omnipotent): Matthew 28:18
10. Eternal: Genesis 21:33; Psalm 90:2
11. Full of Truth: John 14:6
12. Full of Wisdom: Isaiah 11:2
13. Compassionate: Mark 1:41; James 5:11
14. Just: Acts 17:31; Romans 3:25-26
15. Long-suffering: 1 Timothy 1:16; 2 Peter 3:9
16. Kindness: Ephesians 2:7; Titus 3:4-5
17. Gentle: Matthew 21:5; 2 Corinthians 10:1
18. Unchanging (Immutable): Hebrews 13:8; James 1:17
19. Creative: Genesis 1:26; John 1:3; Colossians 1:16
20. Infinite: 1 Kings 8:27
21. Sovereign (Supreme Ruler): Jude 4
22. Unity: Deuteronomy 6:4
23. Full of Goodness: John 10:11; 1 Peter 2:3
24. Trustworthy: Psalm 19:7; Psalm 119:138
25. Generous: 2 Corinthians 8:7-9

PROPHECY BOXES

Pam's Great Expectations

*a*t the age of two, Madison began praying for a baby sister. She wasn't aware that Jerry and I had been praying for another child for over a year. So as a family we were asking God to give us a baby. Months later, when we found out that I was pregnant, we were all excited. Jerry and I had learned through the experience of two miscarriages that a pregnancy didn't always end with a baby to hold on this earth. So we all began praying that God would allow us to have this precious baby.

With the faith of a child, Madison began rearranging her room in anticipation of a little sister. She was ready to share everything from her toys to her shoes. "After all," she told her friends, "God is giving me a baby sister because I prayed."

While I was sick for six months of pregnancy, we kept focused by anticipating what this baby would be like. Our first insight came when a trip to the doctor revealed that the baby was a boy. I wasn't surprised. He had been doing somersaults in my tummy for months. Madison, though, was sure the doctor was mistaken because she had prayed for a girl.

Boy or girl, Madison and I began making plans to dress the baby in precious clothes. That was fine with my husband as long as we followed a few boy rules: no pink, and nothing dainty. Keeping in mind Jerry's manly guidelines, we also brainstormed names, all the while praying for this baby. Finally the day came. On July 7, 1995, the baby we had waited and prayed for arrived—healthy and beautiful. He was indeed destined to be held and loved on this earth. As we cuddled this precious baby boy, we instantly knew Connor Clarkson McCune was the most special baby ever. We never said it to others, but secretly we talked about why our baby was the best. It never occurred to me that emphasizing our story would later complicate the telling of the Christmas story.

It happened three years later as we were celebrating Jesus' birth. I told my children that Jesus was not just any baby but a very special baby. Madison quickly corrected me. "I know all babies are special, but not as special as Connor." I had a problem on my hands. My children would have to be convinced that baby Jesus was a different kind of special. They needed to know more than the who, what, when, and where of the Christmas story. The miracle of this baby was in the *why*. Why was Jesus born? Because God had a plan that was conceived before time began, and He literally moved heaven and earth to see it accomplished. Jesus was the only baby ever born who could save the world. He alone grew up living a sinless life. Therefore, He alone could pay the penalty for our sin by being separated from God on the cross. Jesus was the only baby destined to be the Savior.

Only Jesus fulfilled all the prophecies of the coming Messiah foretold in the Old Testament—where He was born, His escape into Egypt, His ministry in Galilee, His rejection by the Jews, His betrayal by a friend. The list goes on and on. It was no coincidence that Jesus perfectly fulfilled all the prophecies of God. Understanding these truths would set Jesus' birth apart from all others, including Connor's.

We had to find a way to teach these amazing miracles of

God. That's when we added the tradition of Prophecy Boxes. As a family we decorated 25 numbered boxes of various sizes in preparation for our new family tradition. Using spray paint and paint pens, ribbons, and buttons, we decorated each uniquely. In each box I put two different scripture passages. One passage was a prophecy about Jesus from the Old Testament, and the other was the New Testament revelation of Jesus as the fulfillment of that prophecy. Also in each box was a special surprise for the children.

Now each year, beginning December 1, we open one box each night. First the kids retrieve their special surprises from the box, which could be candy or a book. While they are enjoying their surprises, I remind them how nice it is to get the surprise that I had promised earlier in the day. Then we read the prophecy passage in the Old Testament. Each time I explain that "prophecy" means telling ahead of time something that will happen in the future. It's like telling them that they would be getting a surprise later that night and delivering on that promise. In the Bible, God is the one who tells us what will happen in the future. After reading the prophecy, we read its New Testament fulfillment by Jesus.

For 25 days in December, Madison and Connor look forward to opening a new box, finding a surprise, and learning about Jesus. On Christmas day we read the prophecy about His Second Coming and have fun guessing when He might come to fulfill that promise.

If you like the concept behind the Prophecy Boxes, but are not interested in locating, painting, and storing 25 boxes, I have good news. You can also make one Prophecy Box containing 25 envelopes. Instead of a surprise for each day, you can have a special surprise grab bag, or even just a special treat that you reserve only to be eaten when you open an envelope with the verses each day. So don't despair, every family can adapt this way of looking at the special foretelling of God about His Son.

It is a great way, during the busy season, to focus daily on our Savior—His birth, His life, His death, and His resurrection. My children still believe that Connor is special, but because of our use of the Prophecy Boxes, they now know why Jesus is the most precious gift God could ever give us and why only He is worthy of worship.

TIPS FOR PROPHECY BOXES

❋ Visit a hobby store to purchase 25 unfinished craft boxes. You may be able to find nesting boxes that fit inside each other in sets of five or six. On newspaper, set out a collection of craft supplies before your family gathers to decorate them. Among others, supplies might include a glue gun, ribbons, buttons, paint pens, markers, and crayons.

❋ If you plan to spray-paint one base color, do this ahead of time so that the boxes are dry and ready to decorate.

❋ Allow your children to decorate each box with an individual design.

❋ If you would rather, you can prepare all the boxes yourself. If you plan to use them as part of your holiday decorations, you may want to decorate them in a consistent way; for example, all white or all silver with gold ribbon.

❋ Choose a way to number the boxes from 1 to 25. Paint pens work well.

❋ Write out the scriptures or print them on the computer.

❋ You can put the prophecy in the box in several ways. You may glue the prophecy to the lid and the fulfillment to the bottom of the box. You may put it in an envelope in the box, or you could put it on an index card and set it in the box.

❋ Put a surprise for each child in each day's box. This should be something simple and inexpensive. Ideas include a favorite candy treat, stickers, a book, a bookmark, a coupon for a day at the park, a shiny quarter, bubble bath, baseball cards, a coupon to call Grandma and Grandpa, a coupon to pick tomorrow night's dessert, fun pencils, a coupon to stay up 10 minutes later, or a coupon for a ride on Dad's back.

❋ For consistency, open your Prophecy Box at the same time each night, such as after dinner or just before bed.

❋ Provide a grab bag of goodies for the surprise or a special surprise dessert treat just for this time. (We don't recommend desserts just before going to bed, though.)

❋ Each night, after you have read and talked about the passages, praise and worship God together for His great plan to send Jesus to save the world.

❋ There are hundreds of Old Testament prophecies about the Messiah. As you repeat this tradition from year to year, add new passages of prophecy and fulfillment.

Prophecy Box Passages
These passages are from the *Holy Bible: New International Version*. If you have very young children you may want to quote from a children's version.

December 1	Place of birth
	Micah 5:2—You, Bethlehem Ephrathah, though you are small among the clans of Judah, out of you will come for me one who will be ruler over Israel, whose origins are from of old, from ancient times.
	Matthew 2:1—After Jesus was born in Bethlehem in Judea, during the time of King Herod, Magi from the east came to Jerusalem.

December 2   **Heir to the throne of David**
Isaiah 9:7—Of the increase of his government
and peace there will be no end. He will reign
on David's throne and over his kingdom, establishing and upholding it with justice and righteousness from that time on and forever. The
zeal of the LORD Almighty will accomplish this.
Matthew 1:1—A record of the genealogy of
Jesus Christ the son of David, the son of
Abraham.

December 3   **Born of a virgin**
Isaiah 7:14—The LORD himself will give you a
sign: The virgin will be with child and will give
birth to a son, and will call him Immanuel.
Matthew 1:18—This is how the birth of Jesus
Christ came about: His mother Mary was
pledged to be married to Joseph, but before
they came together, she was found to be with
child through the Holy Spirit.

December 4   **Killing of infants**
Jeremiah 31:15—This is what the LORD says;
"A voice is heard in Ramah, mourning and
great weeping, Rachel weeping for her children and refusing to be comforted, because
her children are no more."
Matthew 2:16—When Herod realized that he
had been outwitted by the Magi, he was furi-
ous, and he gave orders to kill all the boys in
Bethlehem and its vicinity who were two years
old and under, in accordance with the time he
had learned from the Magi.

December 5   Escape into Egypt
Hosea 11:1—When Israel was a child, I loved
him, and out of Egypt I called my son.
Matthew 2:14—He [Joseph] got up, took the
child and his mother during the night and left
for Egypt.

December 6   Ministry in Galilee
Isaiah 9:1-2—There will be no more gloom
for those who were in distress. In the past he
humbled the land of Zebulun and the land of
Naphtali, but in the future he will honor
Galilee of the Gentiles, by the way of the sea,
along the Jordan—The people walking in
darkness have seen a great light; on those living in the land of the shadow of death a light
has dawned.
Matthew 4:12-16—When Jesus heard that
John had been put in prison, he returned to
Galilee. Leaving Nazareth, he went and lived
in Capernaum, which was by the lake in the
area of Zebulun and Naphtali—to fulfill what
was said through the prophet Isaiah: "Land of
Zebulun and land of Naphtali, the way to the
sea, along the Jordan, Galilee of the Gentiles—
the people living in darkness have seen a great
light; on those living in the land of the
shadow of death a light has dawned."

December 7   As a prophet
Deuteronomy 18:15—The LORD your God will
raise up for you a prophet like me from among
your own brothers. You must listen to him.

John 6:14—After the people saw the miraculous sign that Jesus did, they began to say, "Surely this is the Prophet who is to come into the world."

December 8   His rejection by Jews
Isaiah 53:3—He was despised and rejected by men, a man of sorrows, and familiar with suffering. Like one from whom men hide their faces he was despised, and we esteemed him not.
John 1:11—He came to that which was his own, but his own did not receive him.

December 9   His characteristics
Isaiah 11:2—The Spirit of the LORD will rest on him—the Spirit of wisdom and of understanding, the Spirit of counsel and of power, the Spirit of knowledge and of the fear of the LORD.
Luke 2:52—Jesus grew in wisdom and stature, and in favor with God and men.

December 10   His triumphal entry
Zechariah 9:9—Rejoice greatly, O Daughter of Zion! Shout, Daughter of Jerusalem! See, your king comes to you, righteous and having salvation, gentle and riding on a donkey, on a colt, the foal of a donkey.
John 12:13-14—They took palm branches and went out to meet him, shouting, "Hosanna!" "Blessed is he who comes in the name of the LORD!" "Blessed is the King of Israel!" Jesus

found a young donkey and sat upon it, as it is written.

December 11   **Betrayed by a friend**
Psalm 41:9—Even my close friend, whom I trusted, he who shared my bread, has lifted up his heel against me.
Mark 14:10—Then Judas Iscariot, one of the Twelve, went to the chief priests to betray Jesus to them.

December 12   **Silent when accused**
Isaiah 53:7—He was oppressed and afflicted, yet he did not open his mouth; he was led like a lamb to the slaughter, and as a sheep before her shearers is silent, so he did not open his mouth.
Matthew 26:60-61—Many false witnesses came forward. Finally two came forward and declared, "This fellow said, 'I am able to destroy the temple of God and rebuild it in three days.'"

December 13   **Struck and spat on**
Isaiah 50:6—I offered my back to those who beat me, my cheeks to those who pulled out my beard; I did not hide my face from mocking and spitting.
Mark 14:65—Some began to spit at him; they blindfolded him, struck him with their fists, and said, "Prophesy!" And the guards took him and beat him.

December 14   Suffered vicariously

Isaiah 53:4-5—Surely he took up our infirmities and carried our sorrows, yet we considered him stricken by God, smitten by him, and afflicted. But he was pierced for our transgressions, he was crushed for our iniquities; the punishment that brought us peace was upon him, and by his wounds we are healed. **Matthew 8:16-17**—When evening came, many who were demon-possessed were brought to him, and he drove out the spirits with a word and healed all the sick. This was to fulfill what was spoken through the prophet Isaiah: "He took up our infirmities and carried our diseases."

December 15   Crucified with sinners

Isaiah 53:12—I will give him a portion among the great, and he will divide the spoils with the strong, because he poured out his life unto death, and was numbered with the transgressors. For he bore the sin of many, and made intercession for the transgressors. **Matthew 27:38**—Two robbers were crucified with him, one on his right and one on his left.

December 16   Hands and feet pierced

Psalm 22:16—Dogs have surrounded me; a band of evil men has encircled me, they have pierced my hands and my feet. **John 20:27**—He said to Thomas, "Put your finger here; see my hands. Reach out your

hand and put it into my side. Stop doubting
and believe."

December 17 **Mocked and insulted**
Psalm 22:6-8—I am a worm and not a man,
scorned by men and despised by the people.
All who see me mock me; they hurl insults,
shaking their heads: "He trusts in the LORD;
let the LORD rescue him. Let him deliver him,
since he delights in him."
Matthew 27:39-40—Those who passed by
hurled insults at him, shaking their heads and
saying, "You who are going to destroy the
temple and build it in three days, save yourself! Come down from the cross, if you are the
Son of God!"

December 18 **Prays for His enemies**
Psalm 109:4—In return for my friendship
they accuse me, but I am a man of prayer.
Luke 23:34—Jesus said, "Father, forgive them,
for they do not know what they are doing."
And they divided up his clothes by casting lots.

December 19 **His side to be pierced**
Zechariah 12:10—I will pour out on the
house of David and the inhabitants of
Jerusalem a spirit of grace and supplication.
They will look on me, the one they have
pierced, and they will mourn for him as one
mourns for an only child, and grieve bitterly
for him as one grieves for a firstborn son.

John 19:34—One of the soldiers pierced Jesus' side with a spear, bringing a sudden flow of blood and water.

December 20   Soldiers cast lots for clothes
Psalm 22:18—They divide my garments among them and cast lots for my clothing.
Mark 15:24—They crucified him. Dividing up his clothes, they cast lots to see what each would get.

December 21   Not a bone to be broken
Psalm 34:20—He protects all his bones, not one of them will be broken.
John 19:33—When they came to Jesus and found that he was already dead, they did not break his legs.

December 22   To be buried with the rich
Isaiah 53:9—He was assigned a grave with the wicked, and with the rich in his death, though he had done no violence, nor was any deceit in his mouth.
Matthew 27:57-60—As evening approached, there came a rich man from Arimathea, named Joseph, who had himself become a disciple of Jesus. Going to Pilate, he asked for Jesus' body, and Pilate ordered that it be given to him. Joseph took the body, wrapped it in a clean linen cloth, and placed it in his own new tomb that he had cut out of the rock. He rolled a big stone in front of the entrance to the tomb and went away.

December 23 **His resurrection**
Psalm 16:10—You will not abandon me to the grave, nor will you let your Holy One see decay.
Matthew 28:9—Suddenly Jesus met them. "Greetings," he said. They came to him, clasped his feet and worshiped him.

December 24 **His ascension**
Psalm 68:18—When you ascended on high, you led captives in your train; you received gifts from men, even from the rebellious—that you, O LORD God, might dwell there.
Luke 24:50-51—When he had led them out to the vicinity of Bethany, he lifted up his hands and blessed them. While he was blessing them, he left them and was taken up into heaven.

December 25 **His Second Coming**
Acts 1:11—"Men of Galilee," they said, "why do you stand here looking into the sky? This same Jesus, who has been taken from you into heaven, will come back in the same way you have seen him go into heaven."
Hebrews 9:28—Christ was sacrificed once to take away the sins of many people; and he will appear a second time, not to bear sin, but to bring salvation to those who are waiting for him.

NATIVITY CENTRAL

Pam's Best Bargain

When people think of Christmas, they often think of a nativity set. The nativity scene takes you back to the first Christmas. You see Mary resting with her first child and Joseph protecting with paternal care. The shepherds are gazing in amazement, while the wise men are bowing down in honor. That simple scene conveys the heart of the Christmas message. Varieties of nativity sets are available for every personality, made in every country, but no matter what language or culture, the nativity scene is universal. It is the language of Christmas.

The first nativity set I ever received was a Precious Moments collectible. Each piece was delicate and sweet. Every season I gingerly wrapped and rewrapped each of the beloved characters and safely tucked them away. At Christmastime I would gently unwrap each piece and display the set in a place of honor.

Eventually, when we had children, that place by necessity got higher. I didn't realize until it was too late that it was not high enough. At the end of the season when I was carefully packing the pieces, I noticed something different about Joseph: His staff was gone. I asked my children about it, and they confessed that when they had secretly played with the nativity set, they had accidentally dropped Joseph, breaking the staff.

Emotionally, I was torn. I loved my special nativity set and wanted it preserved. At the same time, though, I was glad that my children enjoyed playing pretend and reenacting the Christmas story. I compromised. I did impose a "no touching" rule for the Precious Moments set, but I also went shopping for a more durable one.

Searching through all the after-Christmas clearance sales, I found a great nonbreakable crèche for children. I was so excited by my find that I didn't buy just one, I bought two sets. Next season, the kids had their own touchable nativity sets that would soon become their favorite toys. What a joy to watch them reenact that first Christmas as they played the parts with the holy figures. That was what inspired me to look for more.

Now I wanted to see if I could put a nativity set in every room. The hunt was on. Whenever we went on vacations or a ministry trip, we made time to shop for unique nativity sets.

Today I have a wonderful collection of crèches, including a set with three-foot nativity figures. When a local store was going out of business, I found a great treasure hidden upstairs in a corner. There stood a four-foot stable made of old barn wood. My heart raced as I pictured this treasure in my collection. I dashed to the store manager to find out if it was for sale. To my delight, she told me that the stable was just one piece of a whole nativity set made up of three-foot papier-mâché and ceramic figures. My heart soared, and when they finally brought out the whole set, I was in love. I knew I had to have it.

At home, I set about finding the perfect place to display my almost life-sized Mary, Joseph, baby Jesus, and wise men. Its first Christmas season, it migrated from place to place, never quite settling anywhere until it did find a permanent home. Every Christmas, Mary, Joseph, Jesus, and the three wise men look down on our family, literally, from their perch on top of the living room armoire.

Now, as I enter each room in our house, I see a different nativity that reminds me to celebrate Jesus. The figures remind me to give Him thanks for choosing to come to earth as a Child, choosing to die for my sin, and choosing to accept me. What started as a collection is now an interactive worship experience. In the pages that follow, I bet you will find one or two ideas that will transform your family's nativity from a decoration to a devotion that helps you worship our King.

TIPS FOR MAKING THE NATIVITY CENTRAL

✳ If you don't already have one, obtain a nonbreakable nativity set for your children to play with.

✳ Place a nativity set in the center of your family dining table as a reminder to praise and thank God for some aspect of His plan that brought Jesus to the manger. For example: thank Him that Jesus gave up heaven to come to earth; thank Him for Mary who obeyed the angel; thank Him for Joseph's willingness to marry Mary; thank God for protecting Jesus from Herod.

✳ Place a nativity under the tree beside the gifts to remind your family that Jesus is the first and greatest gift of Christmas.

✳ Create a nativity Christmas tree by using only ornaments that symbolize events of the first Christmas. This could be a small tree in a bedroom, a wreath on the door, or your large family tree. Ornaments would include stars, angels, shepherds, wise men, candy-cane staffs, crowns, stable animals, and sheep.

✳ Another idea is to move Mary and Joseph around the house as they travel to Bethlehem. Let your children look for them on their journey. Leave a treat at each new stop along the way for your children to find. Set baby Jesus out with Mary and Joseph on Christmas morning.

❋ Find a set with 25 pieces and bring out one new piece each day, beginning December first.

❋ Tell the Christmas story over a period of seven days by placing the appropriate pieces in the manger as your read the corresponding verses from the Bible. Day 1: Place Mary and read Luke 1:26-38. Day 2: Place Joseph and read Matthew 1:19-25. Day 3: Place the donkey and read Luke 2:1-5. Day 4: Place baby Jesus and read Luke 2:6-7. Day 5: Place the shepherds and read Luke 2:8-12, 15-18. Day 6: Place the angel and read Luke 2:13-14. Day 7: Place the wise men and read Matthew 2:1-12.

❋ Let your children help prepare a manger for baby Jesus. Set out a small wooden manger beside your tree. Jerry made one from pine two-by-fours, but even a cardboard box will work. Set a basket of straw beside it. Each time someone in the family says an encouraging word or does a kind deed, allow him or her to soften Jesus' bed with a piece of straw. Do this throughout December. On Christmas morning, before your children awake, place a doll wrapped in a plain blanket in the manger to represent Jesus. You will find that your children may be as excited about finding Him there as they are about seeing what goodies have been left. Allow them to play with this baby Jesus doll the whole day, but then put it away again until next Christmas to keep it special.

❋ Place a different type of nativity set in every room of the house to keep the family focused on the gift that God sent that first Christmas.

❋ If you collect sets from other countries, use them as a reminder that Jesus offers salvation to all people. Pray for the people of those other countries to receive Christ.

THANK-YOU
JESUS CARDS

Minding Your Manners with Kim

*D*o you know the proper way to say thank you? This is not the usual dinner-party icebreaker, but that was the question our hostess posed at one holiday get-together. She had received a letter from a family member who was concerned that appreciation was not being properly expressed within their family. The offended in-law circulated new guidelines she wished to implement. Our hostess wanted some objective input on the specific new rules.

First, the in-law was adamant in her opinion that e-mail thank-you notes "should not count," since they are too impersonal. Second, mailed notes should be handwritten because they are "more heartwarming." Finally, children should not be exempt from the duty of giving handwritten thanks, since such correspondence is "high on the list of behaviors we must do."

Needless to say, her directives collided with more than a few opinions at our table. These ranged from wholehearted agreement to thank-you note rebellion, with shades of conviction in between. The more we discussed the topic, the more questions were raised. For instance, if I express thanks to someone in person, is a written thank-you note also expected? How long do I have before it is too late to send a thank-you note? Is there an appropriate way to say thanks to someone who sent a gift you returned to the store?

With the gift-giving season looming around the corner, I felt I should find answers to these pressing questions. So I took a ride on the information superhighway. My search for thank-you notes yielded 34,254,331 websites. That is not a misprint. More than 34 million folks are ready to tell me how to say thank you. Admittedly, I only scanned the first 250 entries (I couldn't even spell "thank you" after that), but that was more than enough to reveal that I had much to learn about thank-you note protocol.

As it turns out, all of the experts on manners agree that it is always the right time to send written notes of appreciation. That's bad news for those who were hoping for some exceptions. Not even verbal thanks supersede the carefully penned note. Apparently, a first-class stamp on a greeting card really is worth a thousand words. But don't think it's that easy. Some restrictions do apply. "Never, never, never," I quote, "send a preprinted thank-you card without a personal notation inside." Handwritten somehow implies sincerity. And remember, a truly sincere note will use the pronoun "you" much more often than "I."

"Kim was delighted with the hand-knitted socks you gave her. Each time she pulls them on, she will think of you. You have made Kim's holiday very special. Kim appreciates you, you, you."

Disagreement arises when it comes to time limits on getting those cards and letters mailed. While most agree that acts of kindness, birthday gifts, and the like should be acknowledged within days, wedding gifts are controversial. One advisor says you have up to a year, while another gives just two weeks. Sounds like an argument for a daytime talk show to me.

And what about that gift you took back? The key here is diplomacy. Uncle Willard will be pleased when you tell him that you found the perfect place for the ceramic donkey. Just don't tell him that place was back on the store shelf. In such cases, the advice is "keep it brief."

You may be wondering who should be writing these notes. One expert said, "As soon as a child can manipulate a crayon, she can participate in thanking people." So get that kid out of the high chair and get him practicing the alphabet. Just don't tell the other expert who says that proper notes are always written in blue or black ink, never Parrot-Pink Crayola.

The last word on protocol should go to the quintessential expert on manners, Abigail Van Buren. One reader complained that accepting gifts should not carry unwanted obligations, like thank-you notes. Dear Abby responded, "Accepting a gift *does* create an obligation—the obligation to express appreciation."

God put it another way. "In everything give thanks; for this is God's will for you in Christ Jesus" (1 Thessalonians 5:18, NASB).

Christmas is a perfect opportunity to teach our children to give thanks for all the good and perfect gifts that come down from the Father. In our family, we do this by writing the very first thank-you card of the season to Jesus. After all, He is our greatest gift. And He gives the greatest gifts.

We try to help each of our children recall the things that Jesus has given throughout the past year. Some of the things my children have thanked Him for are Christian friends, a helpful teacher, courage to try out for a play, finding a lost cat, a healthy family, red hair, grandparents, a good pitching arm, a home, brothers, chocolate (oops, that was mine).

There are three areas we ask the kids to think about when they are writing our thank-you card. What are the gifts Jesus has given that you can see and hold? What are the gifts Jesus has given that you can only feel? What are the gifts Jesus has promised to give you in the future? When each person has finished with the card, including my husband and me, we sit in a circle and read each one to Jesus as a prayer.

Thank-You Jesus Cards can be one of your holiday highlights, but remember, your goal isn't to do it all. Balance your holiday with just an idea or two from each section of this book. This is a good one to consider if a night of thanksgiving is just what your family needs to savor the goodness of our Lord.

TIPS FOR WRITING THANK-YOU JESUS CARDS

❋ Choose an evening when your entire family is together and you are not rushed for time.

❋ Your children will enjoy using special colored pens, decorative stationery, and even stickers or stamps. Set these out before you gather to begin.

❋ Choose appropriate passages from Scripture that show God is pleased with a thankful heart. Read these aloud before getting started.

❋ For younger children, prepare a cheat sheet that will help them think about the different gifts Jesus gives. Your older children may want to use it too.

❋ Play praise music or Christmas songs while the thank-you cards are being written.

❋ You may want to have a plate of treats to munch on while everyone works.

❋ Not everyone will finish at the same time, so plan to have puzzles, coloring books, or things to read already set out. This will keep things quiet while others are thinking and writing.

❋ When everyone is finished, turn the music off, unless it is instrumental. If it's left on, turn the volume low.

❋ Start with the youngest and allow each person to read his or her thank-you card to Jesus as a prayer. If there is something personal on someone's thank-you card, be sure he or she has the freedom to keep that private.

❋ Emphasize that thanking Jesus is a way to praise Him. The cards are for Him, not to show off to others.

❋ Don't criticize the length of any card. Some may be short, others long. Affirm each one as an acceptable sacrifice of praise to God.

❋ Allow the head of the household to go last, finishing with a general prayer of thanks for the whole family.

CHRISTMAS CAMPFIRE

Turning Chores into S'mores at Kim's

*O*ne of my children's least favorite chores is picking up
sticks. Our house is located on three acres with many
trees dotting the property. That means lots of sticks and
branches regularly litter the yard. Occasionally these sticks
become so abundant that they must be removed. It only seems
fair that since the kids are lower to the ground, they should get
the assignment. The only job they dislike more is changing the
guinea pig's litter pan.

A few years back, after an afternoon of complaining about
the job, I thought of an idea I hoped would change their attitude. "I've got a proposition for you," I announced. "If you
pick up all the sticks in the yard without complaining, and pile
them all in one stack, I will reward you tonight with a campfire party. We'll have hot chocolate, roast marshmallows, and
tell campfire stories. But you have to work without any more
complaining. And remember, the size of the fire will depend on
how many sticks you gather."

Suddenly, what was a chore became preparations for a
party. They loved the idea. From then on, they eagerly hunted
for every stick they could find, even breaking off branches
from trees that lined the edge of the woods. They weren't planning on a campfire; they wanted a bonfire. They worked

through the entire afternoon until eventually I made them stop for dinner.

When it finally got dark, we each took a lawn chair and made a circle around the sticks, then my husband lit the fire. It was a wonderful night of family fun. We told stories, sang, and roasted marshmallows. My husband told his usual "When I was kid" stories, and we had fun groaning at his absurd exaggerations. This time he told us, "Yep, when I was a boy we were so poor my dad earned just five dollars a week and all the cotton we could eat." All the while, our two youngest, Bailey and Hannah, kept adding leaves and sticks to an already blazing fire. Inspired by a handful of dead leaves that he had picked up, Bailey thoughtfully gave us a family devotion.

"Look, everybody, do you see these dead leaves?" he said as he passed them around for us to feel. "These are all dry and crumbly and falling apart. That's how we are without Jesus." Then he walked over to a bush and pulled a green leaf off of the branch.

"But feel this one," he said. "It's soft and green and alive. That is what our hearts are like when we trust in Jesus." His words were so serious and thoughtful that we were all drawn to what he was saying.

Wow! It was amazing what a little work did for my children. What I had planned as a reward for chores, God had redeemed through my eight-year-old son. Not only did we have a fun family night, but we were also able to focus on the goodness of God in providing us with a Savior. We ended our night by the fire with a prayer of thanksgiving.

By the time the yard filled with sticks again, it was a few days before Christmas. This time, though, I didn't have to ask twice to get help. The kids knew that a stick pile meant a campfire. While they worked, I thought about how meaningful the last one had been because of Bailey's spontaneous devotional. I knew, though, that I couldn't guarantee a repeat performance. Bailey is not prone to regular outbursts of theological exposition. That particular night had been a "God thing." Still, I wanted the next campfire to be just as special. So I decided this time, it would be my turn to have a plan. What resulted was so special that it has become a regular Christmas tradition for our family.

After dinner, we all moved our chairs into a circle around the campfire. I brought out hot chocolate, and for a little while we laughed and told funny stories while we roasted marshmallows over the fire. When all the wiggles and giggles were out, we had a wonderful time of singing Christmas hymns. When we had sung everyone's favorites, I opened my Bible and told them the story of the traveling magi from Matthew 2:1-12.

"Long ago, in a land far away, three men sat huddled around a fire wondering how much longer their journey would take. You see, they were not sure where they were going. All they knew was that they were following a star and looking for a King.

"They knew that God had foretold that His own King, the King of the Jews, was somehow connected to this strange and unusual star. So they set out to find Him. Their journey led them from their home in the east to Jerusalem, the capitol city of the Jews, where they met the king of that land, Herod. 'Where is He who has been born King of the Jews?' they asked. 'For we saw His star in the east and have come to worship Him.'

"When Herod heard this he became upset. He called together his priests who told him the King was to be born in Bethlehem. Herod secretly told the magi, "Go look for him in Bethlehem. And when you find Him, come back and tell me exactly where He is so I can worship Him too.' But Herod really wanted to get rid of Him.

"At last, the magi knew where they were going. They followed the star to the very house where Jesus was. When they saw the Child with his mother, do you know what they did? They fell down and worshiped Him! As they bowed before Jesus, they presented gifts of gold, frankincense, and myrrh. These gifts were precious treasures that they eagerly gave to the Son of God. They gave Him the very best they had.

"When it was time for the magi to leave, God warned them not to go back to Herod, but to go home by another way, so they did. On their way home they probably sat by a fire just like this one and talked about the special Child just like we are doing now.

"Tonight, how about if we give Jesus our treasures the way the magi did? We can give things like obedience or kindness. We can even give up something we do that Jesus doesn't like—perhaps arguing or complaining. I am going to pass around this wrapped gold package. Right now it's empty, but as it comes to you, you can fill it up by giving something from inside of yourself to Jesus. I'll start. I would like to give Jesus my mouth. I want to give it to Him to say kind things; not to complain, but to use it to encourage other people. Hannah, here is the package, what do you want to give Jesus?"

And so the package went around our campfire, into the hands of each person to choose a gift to give to Jesus. When the package made it back to me, I told them I thought it felt very heavy with all the love that we put in it. Then, like the magi, we also bowed down to praise and worship our King in prayer.

The Christmas Campfire is now part of our holiday traditions. It is a great family night to be sure, but more than that, it is a rich time of worship that reminds us that Jesus didn't stay a babe in a manger but came to be our Savior and our King.

TIPS FOR CREATING YOUR CHRISTMAS CAMPFIRE . . . EVEN IF YOU DON'T HAVE A YARD!

❋ If you do not have a yard, or cannot arrange for a campfire, you can still have a Christmas Campfire experience. You can either have your family time around a fireplace or make a "campfire blanket." Place three flashlights under a thin blanket, sheet, or towel. Turn them on, and they will make the blanket glow like a campfire. Turn out all the lights and sit around your "fire."

❋ If you are inside, instead of roasting marshmallows, serve microwave-made s'mores with your hot chocolate.

❋ If you are building a campfire outside, take a few safety precautions. First check with city officials to make sure that there is not a current burn ban in effect. Also inquire if any special permits are required to burn in your yard.

❋ When building your fire, be sure to rake all dry leaves and material in a four-foot diameter around the campfire.

❋ If you have access to sand or rocks, build a perimeter around the sticks.

❋ If you don't have enough sticks, you can purchase firewood from most grocery stores, or you can use a log substitute, such as Duraflame log.

❋ Be sure to go over campfire safety rules with your family before you light the fire.

❋ Never leave children unattended by a campfire.

❋ When you are ready to go in for the night, use a water hose or sand to put out the fire. Check it periodically through the evening to be sure it has not flared back up again.

❋ If you roast marshmallows, have roasting sticks ready before you start. Wire clothes hangers or metal shish kebab skewers work well.

❋ Set out blankets or towels for your family to kneel on during your prayers of worship.

❋ If your family is going to "give treasures to Jesus," wrap a small package in gold paper. If possible, to make it special, add a gold ribbon as well. This will be the package that you pass around. When it gets to each person, that one will get to tell what gift he or she wants to give Jesus.

❋ If your denomination traditionally celebrates the story of the magi as Epiphany in January, you may want to save your campfire until then.

❋ If you do this tradition every year, you can use other "gift" passages for your devotion. See John 12, the story of Mary's gift of perfume to Jesus. You can also talk about all the gifts God has given us, such as the Holy Spirit, eternal life, and grace.

THE GOOD AND PERFECT GIFT

Kim's Island of Misfit Toys

I am not a good gift giver. I never know what the other person would truly want or need. Ask me to baby-sit your kids or donate my kidney, but please don't expect me to give you a thoughtful gift.

Good gift givers like Pam are people who notice details. They remember when you mentioned your favorite flavor of coffee. I can't remember if you even drink coffee. They noticed that you collect chickens. I thought you said you raised chickens. They remember your birthday a week ahead of time. I stop at the store on the way to your birthday party.

As much as I love the holiday season, trying to find the perfect gifts for multiple people is sheer torture. The only thing that keeps me from spontaneously combusting is that, by mutual consent, the adults in our family no longer shop for one another.

Instead, we spend the week before Christmas helping the kids make the gifts they will give to aunts and uncles, grandmas and grandpas. While I am equally unequipped for that task, the majority of the effort comes from the kids. They have masterfully made such things as custom-decorated TV trays, potholders, and photo frames. They have created artful silk ties and scarves and my all-time favorite—tie-dyed shirts and socks. Grandpa Cliff loved his socks so much, wearing them whenever we came to visit, we made sure that when he left us to meet Jesus face-to-face he was wearing them. Grandma Tera loved the gifts so much they always got the most prominent and honored place in her home. Grandparents' pride in their gifts leaves a lasting legacy in my children's hearts. It brings them great joy to give the things they have made. They become giddy with anticipation as their gifts are opened, and they are never disappointed with the reactions. Grandpa John always says, "Oh, will you looky here. How wonderful!" Grandpa Red examines the gifts as if he has never seen anything quite so amazing. Grandma Linda always gets them to explain exactly how the gift was made. And Grandpa Charlie usually says, "I've been needing one of those," even if "one of those" is a psychedelic trinket box.

Even though we make gifts for family, I still have to buy gifts for my children. I live with them and still don't always know what they would like. I have found that the only surefire way to know a gift will be a hit is to give them something living. From tarantulas to bunnies, living, breathing Christmas presents are always a success. Unfortunately, my husband has the final say on the critter collection, and a pet in every package is not an option. I am forced to do some real shopping.

Sometimes I get lucky and choose a gift my kids love, like the lava lamp and the sleeping bags. And sometimes I'm not so lucky. We have a cabinet full of gift mistakes. I now know that my children are not interested in chemistry sets, Barbie dolls, pogo sticks, stationery, modeling clay, journals, and many other items that will soon be in a garage sale.

Each year as Christmas approaches, we look forward to all the special (and not-so-special) gifts that will be under the tree. Each one represents the love and affection we feel for one another. When the last gifts have been given out and the last thank-yous said, there is always one unclaimed package remaining under the tree. Its tag simply reads, "To all who will receive." This is the package we call the Good and Perfect Gift. It is the one gift under the tree that is sure not to disappoint.

When someone finally notices the lone package, it is carried to the center of the room and opened by the eldest member of the family. He reaches in to take out a letter and reads it aloud.

> "To all who will receive: 'Every good and perfect gift is from above, coming down from the Father of heavenly lights, who does not change like shifting shadows' (James 1:17). 'Your Father knows what you need before you ask him' (Matthew 6:8). 'His divine power has given us everything we need for life and godliness through our knowledge of him who called us by his own glory and goodness' (2 Peter 1:3). 'Therefore let us draw near with confidence to the throne of grace" (Hebrews 4:16).

The children are then asked, "Who wants to draw near to find out what good and perfect gift God has given to us?" Each child is allowed to take out one item from the box, such as a small crown. We all try to guess which of God's good gifts it represents before we read the verse that is tied to it with a ribbon. In our box the crown represents the crown of life "promised to those who love him" (James 1:12). It could also stand for "the unfading crown of glory" that we will receive when the Chief Shepherd appears (1 Peter 5:4).

Each year the box contains seven good and perfect gifts God has promised to all those who would receive them through His Son, Jesus Christ. One by one, we take them out and talk about the divine gifts we have in God. It is a wonderful time of focusing our gift-giving tradition on the worship of our Savior. His good gifts outshine anything this world has to offer and are always exactly what we need.

TIPS FOR MAKING THE GOOD AND PERFECT GIFT BOX

❋ Find a box with a removable lid, about the size of a shoe box or larger.

❋ Wrap this box in special paper—gold, if possible.

❋ Inside the box, place seven items to represent the "good and perfect gifts" God says are ours through Jesus Christ. Many of these items you can find at a craft store in the ornament section. There are many other gifts that God has given us. Use the ones below or create your own. Choose some gifts that we have in the here and now and some that we are promised in the future.

> • A crown—the crown of life (James 1:12)
> • An eraser—God's forgiveness of our sins (1 John 1:9)
> • A small doll pillow—God's comfort
>   (2 Corinthians 1:3-4)
> • A small house—our mansion in heaven (John 14:2)
> • Play telephone—the gift of prayer (Ephesians 2:18)
> • Shield—protection (2 Thessalonians 3:3)
> • Bag of plastic jewels or gold coins—treasures in heaven (Matthew 6:20)
> • Lightbulb—the mind of Christ (1 Corinthians 2:16)
> • A box of matches—the Holy Spirit (Ephesians 1:13)
> • Heart—a new heart (Ezekiel 11:19)
> • Homemade adoption certificate—adoption as God's sons (Ephesians 1:5)
> • A homemade diploma—wisdom (James 1:5)

❋ Write the corresponding verse for each gift on a tag and attach it with a ribbon.

❋ Place the lid on the box. Put a tag on the box that says, "To all who would receive."

❋ Place the Good and Perfect Gift Box under the tree with the other packages. Do not indicate to your children that this package is any different from the others.

❋ After all the packages have been opened, someone will notice there is still one present left under the tree. If the children do not notice, one of the parents can point it out. (A note of caution: If you have young children and gift opening is already a long affair, choose a separate time for this tradition.)

❋ Allow the eldest family member to read the tag and open the box. He or she should remove the letter and read it aloud.

❋ Let each child reach in the box and take out one item. Before you read the verse, let them try to guess from looking at the "gift" what good thing God has given.

❋ One by one, take the articles out of the box and talk about these good gifts. Discuss how you have received some and imagine together what it will be like to receive the others in heaven.

❋ End with a prayer, thanking God for being a good and generous Father. Acknowledge that none of the wonderful material packages you opened could compare to the spiritual gifts of Jesus Christ.

❋ From year to year, change the gifts in the box so it will still be a surprise. Put in seven new items that represent seven different gifts.

❋ Take this box with you when you travel for Christmas. Put it under your host family's tree and let them enjoy the tradition.

❋ Make boxes to give away to others at Christmas. You can even leave them anonymously on doorsteps on Christmas.

Other ways to Savor the Savior on Christmas Eve and Christmas day:

❉ Read the Christmas story from Luke 2.

❉ Encourage your children to creatively present the Christmas story for the adults. You may need to help them plan ahead. We have done this with pop-up books, sock puppet shows, and skits.

❉ Attend a candlelight church service.

❉ Light candles at home and sing Christmas hymns such as "Silent Night," "O Little Town of Bethlehem," or praise songs.

❉ Light candles on a birthday cake in honor of Jesus.

❉ Watch *The Jesus Film* or *The Jesus Film for Children,* produced by Campus Crusade for Christ, or another age-appropriate, Christ-focused movie.

❉ Before you enjoy the tradition of giving gifts, allow each person to tell why he or she is thankful to God. Each person may want to share blessings that God has given in the past year. Finish with the reading of James 1:17: "Every good thing given and every perfect gift is from above, coming down from the Father of lights, with whom there is no variation or shifting shadow" (NASB).

❉ Set aside a special time on Christmas night to read the prophecies of Jesus' Second Coming. Pray together as a family for that day to come quickly.

REDEEMING YOUR HEART

What can I give him,
poor as I am?
If I were a shepherd,
I would bring a lamb;
If I were a wise man,
I would do my part;
Yet what I can I give him?
Give my heart.
> —from "In the Bleak Midwinter"
> by CHRISTINA G. ROSSETTI

*C*hristmas is a season full of potential. If used wisely, it will bring great profit. Retailers have certainly figured out the profit angle. Holiday departments spring up in early September before the back-to-school aisles have even been ransacked. Christmas music assaults shoppers who, just moments before entering the store, were enjoying the warm breezes of late summer. Still the music plays on as the aisles are stocked and restocked with holiday goodies. Though candy canes and angel toppers on Labor Day seem premature to us, retailers know that the earlier they invest, the greater their Christmas profits will be.

In the same way, a fulfilling and spiritually rewarding Christmas begins with a personal investment made before the first ornament is taken out of the box. Redeeming the season for ourselves and our families begins when we first allow Christ to redeem our hearts. That happens when we realize that Christ died not only as the payment for our sins but also so that we might live a life transformed by His presence in it. It is Christ alone, and our relationship to Him, that should define the significance of everything else we do.

When we forget that, we risk becoming so entangled in our circumstances that our lives cannot belong fully to Christ because there is no time left over for Him. A redeemed heart is one that does not let that happen but instead sets daily priorities according to that relationship. A redeemed heart says, "Nothing will come between me and Jesus, not carpools nor telemarketers nor PTA projects nor dirty diapers nor demanding bosses nor sheer exhaustion nor any created thing." But is it truly possible to make that a reality?

It is, and there is a woman who can show us what a life lived by these right priorities looks like. Mary of Bethany knew what it meant to have her life and her heart redeemed. This is a woman who understood what was available to her through a relationship with Jesus Christ. As her heart is revealed through her actions, it is evident that she chose a life of devotion instead of a life of distraction. As we look at one incident in her life, we will discover that we can make that same choice.

Mary was the sister of Martha and Lazarus. She lived in the town of Bethany, a frequent stop for Jesus. At the time of this story, Jesus was in His last period of ministry. Luke 9:51 tells us that "when the days were approaching for His ascension, . . . He was determined to go to Jerusalem" (NASB). In some short six months, our Lord would endure the cross. Sometime between that final October and December, Jesus came to dinner at Martha's house.

Thanksgiving and Christmas were not on the seasonal calendar back then, but the Jews were celebrating their holidays, the Feast of Booths and the Feast of Dedication. Like our holidays, theirs involved traveling and an abundance of good food. We don't know the exact day when Jesus came to

Martha's, but I like to imagine that, given her anxieties, it might have been during the holidays. Of course, there would not have been strings of lights on the house, but I could see someone like Martha adding creative touches here and there. From the way Scripture describes her, this hostess with the mostess could have had a papyrus newsletter, "The Martha of Bethany First-Century Guide to Entertaining." I'm sure it would have had great ideas for making centerpieces out of hyssop and removing wine stains with camel spit. With Jesus on His way, her home would have been buzzing with preparations.

The story goes on: "Now as they [Jesus and His disciples] were traveling along, He entered a village [Bethany]; and a woman named Martha welcomed Him into her home" (Luke 10:38, NASB). Since there are no Bethany *Better Homes and Gardens* archives, we have to guess what Martha's home was like. She was able to entertain Jesus and His 12 disciples (and possibly others who followed Him), so we can assume her home was not one of modest means. It might not have been like Beverly Hills, but it certainly wasn't Pigeon Holler, either. In fact, we might conclude that she had servants. There is no mention of her husband, so perhaps she was a widow. Other passages in Scripture indicate that Jesus was fond of this well respected and prominent family. Since Jesus often sent word ahead of His arrival in a town, I think Martha knew He was coming and had big plans for everything to be perfect. I imagine it this way: It was evening, and all the guests arrived together, walking past the special candles that Martha had carefully set out to light the path. When the knock came at the door, Martha was surprised. She had gotten so caught up in the planning that time had slipped away. As she walked to the door, she smoothed down her hair, straightened her gown, and took a deep breath. The guest of honor had arrived.

When she welcomed Jesus and His friends, she genuinely gushed with pleasure to see them. She invited her guests to recline comfortably on the freshly cleaned varicolored rugs and hand-stitched floor pillows that leaned at just the right angle along the wall. The room, of course, was spotless. The smell of food was in the air and servants were on hand to offer a refreshing drink.

Martha herself did not stay long in the room, for as often happens, the guests arrived before everything was complete. As she bustled off to the kitchen to supervise the meal, she left Jesus. As she hurried off, her guest of honor was already sharing His thoughts with those gathered. One was Mary.

The Scriptures tell us, "She [Martha] had a sister called Mary, who was seated at the LORD'S feet, listening to His word" (Luke 10:39, NASB). If Mary was anything like her sister, she was ready to help whenever she was asked. Before the guests arrived, she too, would have been plumping pillows, shaking rugs, and kneading bread. Like Martha, Mary would also have been in the last-minute throes of preparation when the knock came. It was after the door opened that we begin to see the difference.

As Martha made everyone comfortable so she could settle back into the business of entertaining, Mary settled at the feet of the Lord. When He began speaking, Martha turned her attention to other things, but Mary was "listening to His word." She wasn't just hearing Him, she was considering all that He had to say. Mary didn't want to miss even the smallest detail, so she put herself at His very feet so that she could not only hear the words but also experience the expressions on His face, the emotions in His voice, and the intensity of His passion.

"But Martha was distracted with all her preparations" (Luke 10:40, NASB). Eventually, Martha looked up long enough to realize that Mary had not followed her into the kitchen. I imagine her peeking around the corner to see what could have happened to her usually responsible sister. What a shock it must have been to see Mary, lounging with the guests when there was so much work yet to be done. Martha went back to the kitchen and stewed about the situation. The more she thought about all the work she had to do, the harder she pounded the dough on the table. Soon her indignation got the better of her and she peeked around the corner again. She might have tried to get Mary's attention, but of course Mary never looked away from the face of Jesus. *What is that girl staring at,* Martha might have wondered. Determined to rectify the situation, Martha burst into the room and interrupted Jesus as He was speaking. "She came up to Him and said, 'LORD, do You not care that my sister has left me to do all the serving alone? Then tell her to help me'" (Luke 10:40, NASB).

Well, that probably felt good. I imagine she tossed Mary a look that said, "Now you're going to get it!" After all, there were many things that needed to be done. It was irresponsible and lazy of Mary not to help. It was for her sister's own good that she be reprimanded and told to get busy with the important things. By taking it to Jesus, she was hoping for a speedy and decisive resolution—and that is exactly what she got. "But the Lord answered and said to her, 'Martha, Martha, . . . you are worried and bothered about so many things; but only one thing is necessary'" (Luke 10:41-42).

Can you see the indignation on her face? She had worked so hard to make the night special. The time and the expense she had invested were important to her. So important, in fact, that she had interrupted Jesus to vent her frustration. She had put her heart into all of the details, and now Jesus was saying that only one thing was needed. She probably wondered to herself, *How can I serve a house full of guests on one thing? What could that be? The fish, the bread, or the wine?* What one thing did He mean was needed?

Jesus explained, "Mary has chosen the good part, which shall not be taken away from her" (Luke 10:42, NASB).

I can see the confusion on Martha's face. What had Mary done but sit around? As her eyes fell on the face of her sister, who hadn't said a word in her own defense, she saw that Mary was still drinking in every word that the Teacher had to say. She wasn't worried or bothered, as Jesus had rightly described Martha. Mary was doing only one thing—focusing on the Lord Jesus Christ.

As Martha went back to the kitchen alone, I wonder if she evaluated her priorities against the "good part" that was Mary's. Jesus said Martha had chosen as her part a preoccupation with "many things." And though He was gentle, He rebuked her for being so shortsighted.

Yes, she had welcomed Him in, as we do at salvation, but she had not made Him a priority over all other things. Her life had been redeemed, but she was living under the power of the world's entanglements and her heart was still her own. She had yet to give it as Christ's possession.

Mary chose differently. She knew that the best dish at the table was time spent with Jesus. He was her bread, and to her that bread was life. When this bread came within her reach, she took it eagerly, not wanting to miss her opportunity. Martha might have been content to catch a word now and then, but Mary wanted to digest every thought, every nuance, and every breath of the Master's teaching. At His feet, she readied herself to receive whatever Jesus offered. Her heart was set upon the one thing needed.

Like Mary, Martha had a choice, though at first glance she seemed to be in a dilemma. If she focused on her desire to entertain, then she neglected the guest of honor. If she focused on the guest of honor, she would have nothing to feed Him. What could she do, really?

First, let's not forget that this was a woman who probably had many servants attending to the household needs. Martha, it appears, *wanted* to oversee everything personally. She was for much serving. Yet, it was that very serving that made her anxious and bothered. Had she realized the value of time spent at the feet of Jesus, she might have left such things in the care of others.

What if, though, there had been no others with whom to leave it? Certainly in my home, and probably in yours, no one is lining up to serve us. On the contrary, there seems to be no shortage of people lining up to get served. Where do we turn, then, and what other choice could Martha have made?

Twice Jesus had fed thousands with nothing more than a few fish and loaves of bread. Surely, had Martha chosen the one thing needed, the other things would have been taken care of if Jesus had thought them necessary. Consider Matthew 6:32-33: "Your heavenly Father knows that you need all these things. But seek first His kingdom and His righteousness, and all these things will be added to you" (NASB).

I wonder if Martha heard Jesus say those words to the multitude. Had she been listening, or even then had she been busy with her list for tomorrow? If she had been there when He spoke, would she have heard Him say, "Do not worry about tomorrow; for tomorrow will care for itself" (Matthew 6:34, NASB)?

Martha's problem was not with her personality; it was with her priorities. Her care and work were good in their proper place, but the time had come when she had something better to do *first*. Jesus had come to her house seeking fellowship with her and her family. Had she put Him first, she would not have suffered for it—and neither will we.

I don't have to worry that cooking and serving would ever take Jesus' place in my heart—they are already pretty low on my list—but I do have other priorities to consider. Sometimes the phone keeps me from the feet of Jesus. Other times its paying the bills, finishing a book, responding to e-mail, catching a nap, watching the cable news channel, weeding the garden, preparing for my radio show, or lingering just a while longer under the covers. These things all seem necessary, yet they are accomplished at the expense of the one thing I truly need. What things take first place in your heart? If it's not Christ, you may find that, like Martha, you are worried and upset about many things.

Some days I am so burdened by life that it feels as if I have actually been tied up in knots. The pressures I feel as a wife and a mom and a believer are great. Like Martha, and like you, I have fears and heartaches and trials—so did Mary. But she knew where to take all of them. Rather than allowing them to become strings that entangled her, such things were cords that drew her to the feet of Jesus, who had the power to cut them.

What is entangling you? Are you willing to pick it up and take it with you to the feet of Jesus? Will you set your heart on Him and trust that at His feet you will find hope and help and peace? Like Mary, that is where we will hear Jesus proclaim, "She has chosen the good part and it shall not be taken away from her."

Our Lord offers us more than a redeemed season, more than a redeemed life; He offers us a redeemed heart that will change the way we look at everything. It starts by first receiving the redemption at the cross. Without admitting that we need help, that we need to be saved from our sins, we cannot go further with God. The Bible is clear on this: "For all have sinned and fall short of the glory of God" (Romans 3:23). "The wages of sin is death, but the gift of God is eternal life in Christ Jesus our Lord" (Romans 6:23).

Those words were written just for you, for this moment.

With faith, you can be taken from death to life, from the object of wrath to beloved child. Simply tell God that you know it is impossible for you to do enough good things to earn a place in heaven. God's standard is perfection and we all fall short. Confess that you are a sinner in need of a Savior. Then accept the gift of salvation by believing that Christ's death on the cross was the perfect payment for your sin and that His resurrection from the dead proves His promise of eternal life. Just talk to God. Tell Him what is in your heart. You can do that right now!

If you asked, you just received the greatest gift you will ever get! You have Jesus, Himself, and He will never leave you. Pursue Him with your whole heart. Sit at His feet and seek understanding from the Bible. It is His Word, His love letter to you.

For those who have already trusted Jesus, won't you think about giving Him more of your life by setting Him above every other priority?

If like me you have moments of Martha, yet long to live fully as Mary, be encouraged by the wonderful truth that we do have a choice. Our Lord is knocking at your door. Will you welcome Him like Martha, or like Mary? Martha was so much for doing important things that she missed the good part. We don't have to miss it too. The holidays are a wonderful opportunity to evaluate whether we are truly living a redeemed life. Certainly in the midst of the chaos we call Christmas we need our Savior to buy us back from the worries and busyness of the world. It is also a glorious season to put Him first and make worshiping the Savior our great purpose. That is how Christmas can be for a family willing to set aside some of the conventions of the commercial holiday, and instead make an intentional choice to redeem the season.

To those on the outside, a holiday centered on unique family traditions, outreach to others, and significant worship may not make much sense. In contrast to a Christmas primarily

enjoy the journey™

Does parenting sometimes seem like an overwhelming task? Your role as a parent is difficult but very important to you and your children, and Focus on the Family® wants to encourage you! The complimentary Focus on Your Child® membership program has age-specific materials that provide timely encouragement, advice, and information for today's busy parents. With newsletters or audio journals delivered straight to your doorstep once a month and a Web site packed with over 900 articles, Focus on Your Child can help you enjoy the journey!

Here's what the membership includes:

Parenting Newsletters: Four age-specific and concise editions for parents with no spare time.

Audio Journals: Timely information for parents and fun activities for children, based on their ages.

Online Resources: Age-customized articles, e-mail news, recommended resources, and topic-organized forum through which parents can share with one another.

To sign up, go to www.focusonyourchild.com or call (800) A-FAMILY (232-6459).

YF05XPRD

Make Your
Seasons Special
with Resources from Focus on the Family

Christmas in My Heart #14

At the end of the day, gather around the Christmas tree and share these moving stories, from book 14 of the series, that exude the triumph of God's love over wounded hearts and hardship. These stories will capture your heart and hold it spellbound. Don't save them just for Christmas; let them warm your heart year 'round. Hardcover.

Redeeming Halloween

Hoping to get through, get around, or just plain avoid October 31st? It's time to take back Halloween! Celebrate Halloween without selling out! Balance love with conviction, while creating treasured childhood memories for your children. Here is a guide to fun, guilt-free ideas on everything from costumes and decorating hints to original party suggestions. Paperback.

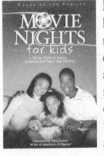

Movie Nights for Kids

Parents and teens everywhere are enjoying fun, yet meaningful, conversations with *Movie Nights*. Now, parents can help their elementary-age children learn to think critically about what they view while they enjoy a good movie with some take-away value. *Movie Night for Kids* zeroes in on the moral heart of 25 entertaining flicks and provides fun, thought-provoking ways to connect, while follow-up activities help your children relate to the moral message of the movie. Paperback.

Meet Kim and Pam through
Engaging Women Ministries

Women Encouraging Women through
Speaking, Writing and Broadcasting

Visit **www.engagingwomen.com**

To discover how this ministry can serve you through:
Retreats and Conferences
Engaging Women Radio Program
Books and Resources
Online Resources

To arrange for Kim and Pam to present a
Redeeming the Season Christmas Event
For your group contact
Engaging Women Ministries
936-560-4888 or info@engagingwomen.com

Other Books Available from Engaging Women

Redeeming Halloween   **Get A Spiritual Life!**   **Are You Talking to Me?**

"A brilliant idea, successfully executed! Anyone interested in grasping key issues in the modern study of New Testament Greek can do no better than read this clear and excellent survey."

—*Moisés Silva*, Retired professor of New Testament, author, and editor

"The complexity, inaccessibility and even hostility of the debates within Greek studies have offered scholars a ready excuse for tuning out and waiting for something useful to come about. And although developments in the last decade have demonstrated potential payoff for exegetes, accessibility to this research in summary form has continued to be a vexing problem until now. Campbell's *Advances in the Study of Greek* stands to deprive even the most cynical reader of the tired excuse that there is nothing new or useful to be learned about Greek. The sweeping overviews of recent discussions, combined with recommended readings at the end of each chapter, enable readers without substantial background to gain a meaningful understanding of the issues, what's at stake, and potential ways forward."

—*Steven E. Runge*, Scholar-in-Residence, Logos Bible Software

"Want to get up to speed on recent research in New Testament Greek? There is no better book (in fact, this is the *only* book!). Con Campbell leads you expertly through the complexities of advances in scholarship so you can be a better teacher, preacher, and student of the Word. Highly recommended!"

—*Andreas J. Köstenberger*, Senior Research Professor of Biblical Theology and New Testament, Southeastern Baptist Theological Seminary

"Campbell takes us on an impressively comprehensive tour of current issues in Greek language study, especially as they relate to the New Testament. The latest in linguistic theory, aspect, deponency, discourse analysis, pronunciation—they are all there, and many more, all covered in an accessible way without compromising standards. The book is above all practical, aiming to bring pastors, teachers and students of Greek to a better understanding of 'what is going on in Greek studies,' as Con puts it. His final plea for a deeper engagement with Greek is compelling: this book is the ideal companion in the endeavor."

—*John A. L. Lee*, Macquarie University

"Students—and even some professors!—whose experience with Koine Greek has been limited primarily to standard elementary and intermediate textbooks, would be astounded to know the height and breadth and depth of work that has been accomplished on the original language of the New Testament in recent years. We live in a time in which great advances are taking place in a variety of directions, but both the specialized nature of the discussions and their relegation to stuffy conference rooms and technical journal articles, have limited the needed impact on frontline Greek pedagogy. Enter Con Campbell, who has provided us with a helpful overview of the history and most salient aspects of paradigm-shifting discussions."

— *George H. Guthrie*, Benjamin W. Perry Professor of Bible,
Union University